D0058628

Confessions of a
White House Ghostwriter

Author of:

Humes, James C.
Confessions of a White
House ghostwriter : five
c1997.
33305008160107
LA   07/29/97

Confessions

of a

White House

Ghostwriter

*Five Presidents and
Other Political Adventures*

James C. Humes

REGNERY PUBLISHING, INC.
Washington, D.C.

SANTA CLARA COUNTY LIBRARY

3 3305 00816 0107

Copyright © 1997 by James C. Hunes

All rights reserved. No part of this publication may be reproduced or transmitted in any form or by any means electronic or mechanical, including photocopy, recording, or any information storage and retrieval system now known or to be invented, without permission in writing from the publisher, except by a reviewer who wishes to quote brief passages in connection with a review written for inclusion in a magazine, newspaper, or broadcast.

Library of Congress Cataloging-in-Publication Data

Published in the United States by
Regnery Publishing, Inc.
An Eagle Publishing Company
422 First Street, SE
Washington, DC 20003

Distributed to the trade by
National Book Network
4720-A Boston Way
Lanham, MD 20706

Printed on acid-free paper
Manufactured in the United States of America

10 9 8 7 6 5 4 3 2 1

Books are available in quantity for promotional or premium use. Write to Director of Special Sales, Regnery Publishing, Inc., 422 First Street, SE, Washington, DC 20003, for information on discounts and terms or call (202) 546-5005.

To Dianne:

In the words of the Bard, "A fine woman, a fair woman, a sweet woman—O the world hath not a sweeter creature."

On the occasion of our fortieth wedding anniversary

CONTENTS

FOREWORD
Rt. Hon. Jonathan Aitken

J ames Humes is "over the top!" The British expression is used to describe a unique character. In a narrow sense, it suggests the reverse of English understatement and reserve, but in a larger sense, it depicts someone with an outstanding personality—in this case, outlandish in style and outrageous in humor.

Of course, Winston Churchill, who is Humes's hero, was "over the top." In 1953, Humes, at that time a student at Stowe School, met the prime minister. "Young man, study, study history, in history lie all the secrets of statecraft."

Humes did, and, like Churchill, he too has had a long love affair with the English language. Yet it is Humes's colorful eccentricity that makes his personality "Churchillian."

I first met Jamie at the opening of the Richard Nixon Library in Yorba Linda in 1990. The former president had recommended that a talk with Jamie might be helpful in the Nixon biography I was then researching.

Any preconception I might have harbored of the former Nixon aide was shattered by my first encounter with this Falstaffian fount of anecdote—from Henry VIII to Henry Kissinger. Humes does not just tell a story—he enacts it, often with the voice and accent of such historical greats as Winston Churchill, Franklin Roosevelt, Lyndon Johnson, or Richard Nixon. Nixon once called him his "Quotes-Master General." His mind is a treasure trove of historical trivia.

One time in 1978, a British author and politician was on an American TV show touting his current novel about an assassination threat to the president. The host asked the English visitor why he wrote about American politics instead of British. "Frankly, very few Americans I come across," answered the Englishman, "know more about American history than I do." The TV interviewer then turned to Humes, who was hawking a book entitled *How to Get Invited to the White House,* and said, "James, why don't you ask our English guest some questions on American history?"

"I wouldn't think of it," said Jamie, "but I will ask him a question about English history: What was the name of the only British prime minister ever assassinated?"

The Englishman stumbled and sputtered "… it's on the tip of my tongue…" and then left the studio in a snit. James gave the answer: Lord Percival in 1814.

Although to an American audience it seemed an easy question, very few Britishers, with the exception of parliamentary historians, would have had the answer on the tips of their tongues. Americans don't realize that there have been four times as many British prime ministers as American presidents—some serving for only a few months.

Only Jamie would have had the knowledge to dredge up the historical nugget and the impish knavery to brandish it and one-upmanship the visiting Englishman.

Shortly after my appointment as chief secretary of the treasury in the John Major's government in 1993, I attended my first session of the Privy Council at Buckingham Palace.

I later described it to Jamie, who relishes hearing every detail of the regalia worn and ritual performed in this vestigial organ of sovereign authority. I further explained that my former deputy in the Defense Ministry was to be made leader of the government in the House of Lords—which thereby entitled him to a seat in the Privy Council. Except that Robert Cecil, as a son of a lord, the marquis of Salisbury—one of the most ancient families in English peerage—

could not advance to the House of Lords before his father's death. Jamie displayed his command of the arcana of aristocracy by bringing up the fact that some of the oldest peerage retained the Right of Acceleration which allowed the son of a lord to advance to a lesser peerage title in the family.

In the ceremonial meeting of the Privy Councillors, Robert Cecil mistakenly took the monarch's seat in the Chamber. Cecil's faux pax, I told Jamie, for some reason provoked a gale of laughter from the queen and Cecil. Jamie then explained why by relating the private joke that the royal family has shared with the Cecil family for four centuries.

When the first Cecil was about to be knighted in 1569, he knelt before Queen Elizabeth but then "broke noisome wind" and retreated without receiving the honor. Twenty years later, when the old chief treasurer was again proposed for a baronetcy, he paused in his advance to the throne. And Queen Elizabeth said, "Have no care, Cecil, I have forgiven the fart."

Winston Churchill once said, "I am a child of the English-Speaking Union." So, strictly speaking, is James Humes, who came to Britain to study at Stowe School on an English-Speaking Union Fellowship. In a year during which he met Churchill and danced with the queen, he incurred a terminal case of Anglophilia.

But his love of Britain and my love of America, as well as our mutual respect for Richard Nixon, were the strands that forged our friendship.

At the opening of the Nixon Library, Jamie took me to a private celebration in a hotel room where old Nixon hands like Bob Haldeman, Herb Klein, and Bob Finch had gathered. He introduced me by saying, "Jonathan, these are Nixon's 'foul weather friends.'" The phrase was one that Churchill used to describe my uncle, Lord Beaverbrook. Well, if James Humes is "over the top," no one can top him as a foul weather friend for the "special relationship" between Britain and America.

PREFACE

I n January 1997, President Bill Clinton delivered his second inaugural address to almost universal derision. It was, agreed most of the critics, an abysmal, pointless speech full of empty phrases, an unappetizing mix of bombast and bromide. The sad thing for President Clinton is that his speech was panned not by a discriminating public that expects works of rhetorical genius as a matter of course, but from a public whose expectations are already miserably low. Americans tend to think the age of eloquence is past.

Maybe it has. But there's no reason why it can't be reborn. Twenty-three centuries ago, Demosthenes, the father of all orators, taught us that a memorable address contains four elements: a great man, a noted occasion, an impelling message, and a superb delivery.

Delivery, of course, can be trained. A message can be honed. Indeed, even ideologically ambiguous politicians like President Clinton are surrounded with advisers to help them define and hammer home a simple message. That's the one irreducible skill a politician must have to get and keep his job.

Occasions for great speeches can be made. There is no reason, for instance, why Ronald Reagan's speech at the D-Day celebrations shouldn't have been forgettable boilerplate patriotism. It wasn't, because President Reagan delivered a great speech about the young U.S. Army Rangers, the boys of Pointe du Hoc, who were now elderly men, many of whom attended the ceremonies. He reminded them and the rest of his audience what it was like that day to leap into history as part of the initial assault for the liberation of Europe. His language was poetic, thrilling, and true. Ronald Reagan's speech made a great occasion.

The one ingredient that speechwriters and speech coaches, spin doctors and press spokesmen can't manipulate is whether their candidate is a great man. When we talk about the absence of great speeches in American political life today, we might really be talking about a much bigger vacancy. It's one thing for a speechwriter to sit facing a blank piece of paper. It's quite another to sit facing a blank piece of paper, having to write a speech for a politician whose character is as erasable as an Etch-A-Sketch.

It may be true that no man is a hero to his valet, but I've been blessed in my experience as a kind of literary valet, as a speechwriter, to work for men I deeply admire. What follows is a sort of autobiography—my life as a mirror to the lives of the great men, the great presidents, for whom I've worked.

I have written speeches for more presidents than anyone, which is the wrong way of saying I'm the most fortunate speechwriter in America today. Here are my confessions, the confessions of a White House Ghostwriter.

—*James Humes*
Washington, D.C.
February 4, 1997

ACKNOWLEDGMENTS

I n just about every autobiography on the market today, the subject—with the egregious exception of First Lady Hillary Clinton—pays tribute to the principal writer. I had the exceeding good fortune to call on the gifted talents of a brilliant, insightful, and sensitive writer who could read the very thoughts from my mind—James Calhoun Humes.

Seriously, in life's journey I owe much to my father's example, my mother's teachings, and the brotherly support of Samuel and Graham Humes, who were the staunchest of friends, as well as brothers.

I have written twenty-one books, but the creations I am most proud of are my two daughters, Mary and Rachel.

As Timon in Shakespeare's *Timon of Athens* said, "I am wealthy in my friends." I honored that wisdom in 1994, at our reception in Washington at the Society of Cincinnati's Anderson House for my Queen's decoration.... I called out to my guests with... apt phrase from the Bard to describe them. I now include those and honor other friends:

Jonathan Aitken, "The courtier's, soldier's, eye, tongue, sword; the expectancy and rose of the fair state"—*Hamlet* Trevor Armbrister, "He is 'A great observer and he looks Quite through the deeds of men'"—*Julius Caesar*; Don Baldwin "Good counsellors lack no clients"—*Measure for Measure*; Samuel Humes Ballam, "Your name is great In mouths of wisest censure; but good faith, I had as lief have been myself alone."—*Othello*; Ken Bolton, "I thank you for your company"—*As You Like It*; Susie Brant, "Teach me, dear creature"—*The Comedy of Errors*; Hugh Bullock, "He is as full of valour as of kindness; Princely in both"—*Henry V*; Josiah Bunting, "That's a brave man! he writes brave verses, speaks brave words, swears brave oaths…"—*As You Like It*; Robert Butera, "In thy face I see The map of honour, truth and loyalty"—*Henry VI* (1); Edward Cox, "So fared our father with his enemies. Methinks, 'tis prize enough to be his son"—*Henry VI* (3); Lord James Crathorne, "I sin in envying his nobility"—*Coriolanus*; Elliot Curson, "His art is of such power"—*The Tempest*; H. Richard Eisenbeis, "The boy was the very staff of my age, my very prop"—*Merchant of Venice*; David Eisenhower, "Who is thy grandfather: he made those clothes, Which, as it seems, make thee"—*Cymbeline*; Tom Evans, "They that thrive well take counsel of their friends"—*Venus and Adonis*; Mickey Feldman, "Fit counsellor and servant for a prince"—*Pericles*; Robert Fredericks, "I do attend here on the general"—*Othello*; Richard Frick, "Smooth runs the water where the brook is deep"—*Henry VI* (2); Dr. Clare Fox, "Beauty and honour in her are so mingled"—*Henry VIII*; David Graham, "As true we are as flesh and blood can be"—*Love's Labour Lost*; Charles Greevy, "O noble judge!"—*Merchant of Venice*; Perrin Hamilton, "Good counsellor"—*Henry VI* (2); George Higham, "The world assurance of a man"—*Hamlet*; Ralph Hooper, "A Bohemian born"—*Measure for Measure*; Jean Humes, "That man i' the world who shall report he has A better wife, let him nought be trusted"—*Henry VIII*; Frank Keenan, "I have great comfort from this fellow"—*The Tempest*; William T. Ketcham, "He is a worthy gentleman"—*Henry IV* (3); Richard Krim, "His nature is too noble for the world"—*Coriolanus*; Jane Krumrine, "A good heart's worth gold"—*Henry IV* (2); Bev Landstreet, "Fly by an eagle"—*Antony and Cleopatra*; John LeBoutillier, "As true a dog as ever fought at head"—*Titus Andronicus*; Richard Lederer, "His words are a very fantastical banquet"—*Much Ado About Nothing*; Dr. Charles Lee, "Me, poorman, my library was dukedom large enough"—*The Tempest*; Margaret Lindemuth, "Women's gentle brain"—*As You Like It*; Thacher Longstreth, "Thy spirits are most tall"—*Henry V*; Eileen and Howard Lund, "As merry As, first, good company, good wine, good welcome"—*Henry VIII*; Charles Manatt, "Can he that speaks with the tongue of an enemy be a good counsellor?"—*Henry VI* (1); Victor Mauk, "An argument of laughter"—*Timon of Athens*; John McClaughry, "There is not such a word Spoke of in Scotland as this term of fear"—*Henry IV* (1); Ambassador Richard McCormack, "Turn him to any cause of policy, the Gordian knot of it he will unloose"—*Henry V*; David McCreery, "The soul of sound good fellowship"—*Troilus and Cressida*; Florence McElroy, "Age cannot wither her, nor custom stale Her infinite variety"—*Anthony and Cleopatra*; Norbert McGettigan, "Monsieur Traveller"—*As You Like It*; Patty Gerber McKernan, "Sunny locks hang on her temples like a golden fleece"—*Merchant of Venice*; Dr. Robert Miller, "Continue this united league"—*Richard III*; Roger Morrow, "All my best is dressing old words new"—*Sonnet 76*; Charles Moyer, "A gentleman of excellent breeding, admirable discourse"—*Merry Wives of Windsor*; Tom O'Neill, "We are advertised by our loving friends"—*Henry VI* (3); Susan Bunting Pierce, "Use a more spacious ceremony to the noble lord"—*All's Well That Ends Well*; John Pierson, "To write and read comes by nature"—*Much Ado About Nothing*; John Price "Honour and policy, [are] like unsever'd friends"—*Coriolanus*; Cecil Quillen III, "A son who is the theme of honour's tongue"—*Henry IV* (1); James Reichley, "A scholar, and a ripe and good one"—*Henry VIII*; Diana Atwood Reilly, "All orators are dumb when beauty pleadeth"—*The Rape of Lucrece*; Permar Richards, "The best king of good fellows"—*Henry V*; James Ring, "[His] heart Is true as steel"—*A Midsummer Night's Dream*; Lewis Robbins, "Remembering my good friends"—*Richard II*; Rod Ross, "There was good sport at his making"—*King Lear*; Dr. Jarvis Ryals, "We are such stuff As dreams are made of"—*The Tempest*; Priscilla Ryan, "If music be the food of love, play on"—*A*

Midsummer Night's Dream; William Schulz, "He knows the game"—*Henry VI* (3); John Scott, "Constant as the northern star"—*Julius Caesar*; Dr. Bob Shirley, "When we mean to build, we first survey the plot, then draw the model"—*Henry IV* (2); Dr. Harvey Sicherman, "The world's mine"—*Merry Wives of Windsor*; Allen Simpson, "I say, put money in thy purse"—*Othello*; Walter Smedley, "There be good fellows in the world, an a man could light on them"—*The Taming of the Shrew*; Jack Smith, "Since every Jack became a gentleman, There's many a gentle person made a Jack"—*Richard III*; Robert Bland Smith, "You are a gentleman and a gamester, sir"—*Love's Labour Lost*; Joe Stevens, "No tricks in [his] plain and simple faith"—*Julius Caesar*; Jack Sweeney, "He is a soldier fit to stand by Caesar"—*Othello*; John Taylor, "The king's name is a tower of strength"—*Richard III;* Dr. Hall Todd, "The churchman bears a bounteous mind indeed"—*Henry VIII*; Granville Toogood, "Mend your speech a little, Lest it may mar your fortunes"—*King Lear*; Judge Robert Van Antwerpen, "That supernal judge, that stirs good thoughts in any breast of strong authority to look into the blots and stains of right"—*King John*; Lew Van Dusen, "Valiant, wise and no doubt, right royal"—*Richard III*; William Vogel, "O wise and upright judge!"—*The Merchant of Venice*; Gen. Charles West, "God's soldier be he!"—*Macbeth*; Robin West, "[A] knavish sprite Call'd Robin Goodfellow"—*A Midsummer's Night Dream*; Don Whitehead, "I am not of that feather to shake off My friend when he must need me"—*Timon of Athens*; Ambassador Faith Whittlesey, "O tiger's heart wrapt in a woman's hide!"—*Henry VI* (3); J. D. Williams, "[He is] meet to be an emperor's counsellor"—*Two Gentlemen of Verona*; Dr. Charles Wolferth, "A giving hand"—*Love's Labour Lost*; John Youngman, Jr., "Do as adversaries do in law, Strive mightily, but eat and drink as friends"—*The Taming of the Shrew.*

Finally, I thank my editor, Trish Bozell, who pared my prolixity.

INTRODUCTION

J amie once told me, "Julie, it's an irony that your father—who was one of the few real thinkers and students of history in politics—was so hated by the intellectuals."

Perhaps the inscribed photograph from my father that I have seen in the Humes's home in Philadelphia was an exchange of mutual respect. "To Jamie, an honest intellectual." To the very end of his life, almost every day my father commented on foreign policy analyses, position papers, or new political ideas that were forwarded or faxed to him by those in and out of government from all parts of the world.

Jamie makes the observation in this book that, "Unlike most politicians, Nixon was more comfortable with ideas than with superficial small talk." I particularly appreciated his statement that the "warmest" president he ever worked with was my father. My father loved the company of bright men and women who were unencumbered by a doctrinaire mindset. He was fascinated with ideas but not by ideologues. Scintillating minds—like those of Pat Moynihan, Henry Kissinger, Bill Safire—received a warm reception from my father because they were not filtered by the blinders of the radically chic or politically correct.

In William Safire's book on the Nixon presidency, he cites from a presidential memo, "Why can't you other writers come up with the parables like Jamie Humes?" My father, who once called Jamie "the Quotes-Master General," often called on his storehouse of historical anecdotes, political lore, and quotations to dramatize or illustrate a point in his speech.

The relationship between the Nixon and the Humes families began back in the late 1950s, when my father was vice president. I say "families" because a special favorite of my father was Jamie's wife, Dianne. She had resigned from the Foreign Service to work in the Eisenhower White House. Then she had left the White House to work for my father. My father used to say that Dianne was his best "message" writer (composing telegrams of greetings for national conventions, and letters of praise, or praise and condolence for some heroic or humanitarian deed).

Receptions for the vice presidential staff brought the newly married Humes couple into our Forest Lane home in Washington. On one occasion, my father was struck by a remark by Jamie that the Hiss case was the root cause of the rancor the academic community harbored toward Nixon. It was Jamie's point that Eastern liberals never forgave my father for being right. My father asked Jamie, then a law student, to write a memo analyzing that hostility, with some recommendations for blunting it. Jamie started then to work part-time for my father in the vice presidential office.

If we left the depiction of presidents to only the Washington corps of journalists, a reader might think Eisenhower was an "amiable boob," Ford a "physical klutz," Reagan a "shallow actor," not to mention the caricature of my father.

In James Humes's books, the presidents and the issues of their day come alive. With robust humor and penetrating insight, James Humes enables the reader to see new and fuller dimensions of the men who have captured the nation's greatest political prize. Humes's Washington odyssey is always entertaining and always enlightening.

Julie Nixon Eisenhower

Chapter One

WHITE HOUSE WORDSMITH

His words are a very fantastical banquet.
MUCH ADO ABOUT NOTHING

T here are illusions—or delusions—about a White House speechwriter. People entertain the illusion of some whiz kid planting notions into the ear of the Great Man. The delusion is that the presidential scribe eventually starts fooling himself that he really has such power.

Actually, the speechwriter is more "image maker" than "idea maker." Back in the early days of the New Deal, the press called some of Franklin Roosevelt's speechwriters—particularly Raymond Moley and Judge Sam Rosenman—"the brain trusters." Well, the speechwriter today is more beautician than brain truster.

Presidents don't want new ideas from their writers. New ideas are controversial ideas. They rattle the status quo. Presidents prefer old clichés that are reminted to seem like brilliant insights.

What is Franklin Roosevelt's most-remembered line? The one in his Inaugural on March 4, 1933. "Let me again assert my firm belief that the only thing we have to fear is fear itself."

FDR could have said, "Don't push the panic button," but that's not very original. Nor would he have made *Bartlett's Quotations* if he had just said, "Have faith." But Sam Rosenman crafted a beautiful line from an old bromide.

Twenty-eight years later, another president in his Inaugural Address captured the imagination of his country when he proclaimed, "Ask not what your country can do for you, ask rather what you can do for your country." Again, speechwriter Ted Sorensen had come up with a ringing way to say "be patriotic."[1]

Read aloud this line by Ray Price, writer for Richard Nixon:

> Faith without strength is futile
> but strength without faith is sterile.

It combines both parallel phrasing and poetic rhyme. As women go to hairdressers to *look* beautiful, presidents count on the speechwriter or word cosmetician to make them *sound* beautiful.

Another notion people have about speechwriters is that they spend most of their time punching out drafts of earthshaking importance—an Inaugural Address or a State of the Union Message. Well, an Inaugural Address is written every four years and the State of the Union every year—not much to keep a stable of six or seven speechwriters busy. Even if you pile the recent ritual of the Saturday radio address[2]—started by Nixon and institutionalized by Reagan—or the occasional speech that the networks televise from the Oval Office, it doesn't add up to a hefty caseload.

Actually, what you do, most of the time, is serve up the same kind of pap that some anonymous scribe in Buckingham Palace does

---

[1] By the way, Sorensen might have borrowed that line from one of the few presidents who wrote most of his own speeches—a former hack journalist who became President Warren Harding. He said in 1923, "We need to be thinking not so much of what the country can do for us but what we can do for our country." A more likely source is Philip St. John, headmaster at Choate in the 1930s, who used to say frequently, "It's not what Choate does for you, but what you can do for Choate."

[2] Franklin Roosevelt, a master of the radio medium, created "The Fireside Chat," but it was an occasional talk, not a regular ritual.

almost every day for Queen Elizabeth. For every inaugural there are thousands of "ceremonials." Peter Benchley used to draft speeches for Lyndon Johnson. (He quit in 1968 to write *Jaws*.) Benchley had a name for these informal remarks—"Rose Garden Rubbish."

That's how Benchley described the concoctions of commendations, felicitations, and salutations that come forth from the president when he exits the Oval Office into the Rose Garden to deliver greetings to the Easter Seal Poster Girl or the "seasonal wishes" when he lights the National Christmas Tree.

Some writers resent their talents being wasted on these ceremonials for the president as chief of state. I didn't! Such "Rose Garden Rubbish" includes toasts at state dinners to visiting royalty as well as presidents and prime ministers. I always liked doing these "chores" for President Nixon because he used to invite the toast-writer to the "coffee and brandy hour" after the state dinner. (That's when guests file into the East Room after their banquet in the State Dining Room.)

Unlike a Queen Elizabeth, the president does not make Frank Sinatra "Sir Francis" or Ted Turner "Earl of Atlanta," but we do have our republican version of knighthood or peerage—the Presidential Medal of Freedom. I once spent a whole day writing one Duke Ellington. "In the royalty of music, no one swings higher than the Duke."

Yet ceremonials shouldn't be lightly dismissed. The greatest American address in history was a ceremonial—the Gettysburg Address. Lincoln, by the way, wrote it himself, and not on the back of envelopes on the train ride to Gettysburg. He sweated out seven drafts in his Executive Mansion study before he was satisfied. (Two words, however, he did ad-lib—he added "...that this nation *under God*...".)

Peggy Noonan, with her Gaelic ear for melodic lines, drafted ceremonials for Reagan. Two which captivated the world were the speech at Normandy in 1984 and the one lamenting the crash of the *Challenger* spaceship in 1986.

Space was also the occasion of my most cosmic contribution. In 1969, I penned my draft for the plaque on the moon vehicle (actually it was on the LEM, the Lunar Expeditionary Module) that was left on the moon:

> Here men from the planet earth first set foot upon
> the moon in July 1969, A.D. We came in peace
> for all mankind.

It would be followed by the names of President Richard Nixon, Edwin Aldrin, Neil Armstrong, and Michael Collins.

Just before submitting it, I dined *al fresco* at an Italian restaurant on 18th & M Streets. I scratched out on a paper napkin these words after two bottles of Chianti.

> Just as man explores space,
> hope unites mankind exalting science.

Of course, the original draft was taken but, when it was pointed out to Bob Haldeman that it was an acronym of my name, I was soon called on the carpet.

"Humes," said Haldeman, "it's sacrilegious, it's obscene—this ego trip."

"Mea culpa," I replied. "If going to the moon doesn't qualify for an ego trip, what does?"

In July 1995, I was regaling my audience with my moon story at one of the camps in Bohemian Grove. As I bragged about "writing on the moon," one listener interrupted, "Jamie, you may have written on the moon, but I walked on the moon." I hadn't realized that a member of my audience of three was Pete Conrad.

I AM ALWAYS ASKED, "Why does a president need to have these

extended amenities written out? Why can't he just wing it?" The answer is that everything the president says is engraved eternally in stone. President Carter tried ad-libbing at a state banquet in Mexico City by saying he had suffered from "Montezuma's revenge" on his honeymoon in Mexico. That almost triggered a rift in relations with our border ally!

When I'm out on the lecture circuit, I get questions from listeners who think there's something dishonest, or at least deceptive, about the use of a speechwriter. But a president has to be both "king" and "prime minister" and wear, as well, all the other hats as chief executive, commander-in-chief, and head of party. If he had to write all his own speeches, he wouldn't have time to do anything else.

By the way, a presidential speechwriter is not a recent development, a reaction to twentieth-century media demand. It dates back to when George Washington was president. He thought he was "an elected king" and the only model he knew was King George III, even though he'd kicked him out of the colonies. Prime ministers like Pitt wrote George III's speeches to Parliament just as Margaret Thatcher and John Major have drafted speeches for Queen Elizabeth for the past fifteen years.

George Washington's famous Farewell Address (the only speech required to be read aloud by Congress each year) was ghosted by Alexander Hamilton.

Of our forty or so presidents, only a few wrote their own speeches, such as Thomas Jefferson, James Madison, Abraham Lincoln, Theodore Roosevelt, and Woodrow Wilson. (By the way, the first presidential speech ever typed out was Lincoln's Second Inaugural in 1865.)

Far from trampling on the Rose Garden requests, I welcomed the chores and cultivated the chance to write them. President Nixon once called me "the schmaltz king" for my declarations and dirges on decorations, disasters, and death.

In 1978, when I was promoting my book *How to Get Invited to the White House,* Tom Brokaw on *Today* asked me, "Mr. Humes, you did a lot of the fluff speeches but not the hard ones?"

I replied, "I don't know about that. You try sometime writing the presidential Thanksgiving Day message and not sounding trite!"

What I didn't tell Brokaw was that it was even harder because I didn't have the journalistic experience that most White House writers have. My equalizer was my arsenal of anecdotes and quotes.

THE FIVE PRESIDENTS I HAVE worked for include all the Republicans since the chief executive at the time of my birth— Herbert Hoover.

I drafted some remarks for Dwight Eisenhower in the last month of his presidency and others in 1967 in connection with the Nixon election effort. But most of my writing was for Nixon—first as a part-timer in his vice presidential office, then in his presidential campaign, and finally in the White House in 1969 and 1970, after which I went over to the State Department. I came back to the White House in 1976 to write some speeches for Gerald Ford. Later, in 1977, I was an editorial adviser in the preparation of his memoirs.

Of the five presidents I worked for, the one with whom I had least contact was Ronald Reagan, which I regretted since he had the best delivery of drafted remarks. Previously, I had helped him with a draft in 1975, while he was still governor of California. And I supplied him with some help in ceremonial toasts and remarks when called on during his presidency.

As for George Bush, I wrote speeches for both of his abortive campaigns in 1980 and 1988. I also supplied some speech material when he was president, in response to requests from the White House.

My life as a White House speechwriter could be said to have begun when I first came to the attention of Vice President Richard Nixon. At the time, my wife Dianne was writing the "Messages" for

Nixon to sign. Those were letters of commendation or condolence, such as the fiftieth anniversary of the VFW or the death of Mrs. Woodrow Wilson.

In a conversation with Nixon at a staff party, I told him of my file of a thousand quotations, as well as the hundreds of anecdotes that I had collected from my readings. I had stacked up to the ceiling in our Capitol Hill apartment ten black looseleaf notebooks that bulged with quotations. They had labels that ranged from "Action" to "Youth," as well as inspirational tidbits amassed from reading biographies such as Sandburg's six volumes on Lincoln or histories such as Will Durant's tomes on the history of civilization, and even the Bible and Shakespeare.

Nixon once introduced me to cabinet member "Red" Blount, saying, "Mr. Postmaster General, James Humes is my Quotes-Master General."

What Nixon liked was that he didn't have to memorize or read the remarks if he had an anecdote on which to play off. Once he got the anecdote in his head, such as the following about Jefferson and Franklin, he could expand it in a few sentences.

> When Thomas Jefferson arrived in 1778 to be our minister to France, the French prime minister Count Vergennes said, "Monsieur Jefferson, have you come to replace Dr. Benjamin Franklin?"
>
> Jefferson replied, "No one could ever replace Doctor Franklin. I am only succeeding him."
>
> And Secretary [So-and-So] can never be replaced...

Bill Safire, in his *Before the Fall,* referred to this when he quoted Nixon: "Why can't you guys come up with the parables like Jamie Humes?"

Or take this tidbit that I dug up from my files—this one from Will Durant—when Nixon was toasting the shah:

The forerunner of Persia was Medea, and the capital
of Medea was Ecbatana. Now Ecbatana means, in Farsi,
a place where people from different religions and
backgrounds meet to discuss peace. And tonight that is
what the shah and I...

In my part-time work for Vice President Nixon in the 1960 campaign, I noted how Kennedy in his campaign speeches would often
end with an important vignette from history. Sorensen, in his book
on JFK, used some of these so often he would just end his draft with
a hand-drawn picture of a "Sun" or "Candle."

If it was a picture of the sun, Kennedy would close this way:

At the Constitutional Convention of 1787, Benjamin
Franklin arose and said, "I have often looked at the
presiding chair which bears the design of a sun low on
the horizon.

"I can tell you that there were months that I thought
it was a setting sun, but today I know it's a rising sun, a
new day for America, a new dawn for freedom."

Or if it was a drawing of a candle, Kennedy would say,

On June 4, 1780, in Hartford, Connecticut, there was
an eclipse of the sun so that even at noon it was as dark
as midnight. In that day—more religious than today—
many thought it was the end of the world.

State legislators in the General Assembly clamored
for adjournment, but the Speaker of the House,
Colonel Davenport, silenced the din with these words,
"Gentleman of the House, the Day of Judgment is
either at hand or it is not at hand. If it is not nigh,
there is no need to adjourn, but if it is at hand, I

would want the Lord to know that I was doing my duty.

"I therefore will entertain the motion that candles be brought in to enlighten this hall of democracy."

My arsenal for ceremonials may have got me into the White House, but no speechwriter likes to admit he spends a lot of time dishing up the Rose Garden Rubbish. He or she prefers to have everyone think that he is formulating presidential policy. In fact, don't look in the White House directory for the Speechwriting Department. It comes under the euphemism Presidential Policy Staff.

But what about the messages to Congress on health care or foreign aid? I am often asked, "Jamie, didn't the president have one speechwriter who was a specialist on welfare and another who was a foreign policy expert?"

To which I would answer, "We writers are translators"—not translating Spanish into English but translating the bureaucratic into the poetic, the legalese into the elegant, the corporatese into the conversational, the complex into the simple.

Speechwriters are generalists—they can't be specialists! If the writer had been an economist or sociologist he'd write that way. The job of the writer is to zap the jargon with which academics or bureaucrats couch their proposals.

New foreign policy positions are drafted by someone in the National Security Council, budget messages by some deputy assistant secretary of the treasury.

But if a president were ever to deliver a televised address in the same form that some department functionary sent over to the White House, it wouldn't be a "Fireside Chat" because it would put out the fire!

In 1942, a civil servant brought, for Franklin Roosevelt's inspection, a new placard that was to be posted in every room of every federal building across the nation. The sign was prompted by the need for blackouts at a time when the United States believed it was threatened by bomb attacks.

The placard read:

IT IS OBLIGATORY TO EXTINGUISH
ALL ILLUMINATION BEFORE THE
PREMISES ARE VACATED.

Roosevelt took one look at it and roared, "Why the hell can't we say 'Put out the lights when you leave'?!"

A speechwriter would also like you to believe that he is some kind of alter-ego for the president. Ted Sorensen for JFK, Bill Moyer for LBJ, Peggy Noonan for Reagan. With the possible exception of Sorensen, Ray Price for Nixon was the only one. (He would become Nixon's "son," the philosophical and ideological extension of the man.)

Actually, the Camelot speeches of JFK manifested more of Sorensen's taste than Kennedy's. Sorensen was a would-be poet who liked to entertain at dinner parties with comic verse and ditties. The internal rhyme in Kennedy's speeches was a Sorensen trademark. ("We prefer world law in an age of self-determination—we reject world war in an age of mass-extermination.")

When people asked me how I managed to work into a Ford style after writing for Nixon, I answered, "I don't try adapting—I write them all the same—simple syntax and conversational style."

It's as if someone were to ask me to bring back a dress from Paris for their daughter who is a size six. I'd buy something with simple lines and let the young woman make it her own with accessories and hairstyle.

A president will make an uncluttered style his own just by his individual inflection and delivery. The only time I ever tried for rhetorical eloquence was in an inaugural or convention acceptance speech which I knew the president would rehearse many times. If a president is reading a prepared text without at least reading it over several times, he is more likely than not to stumble over an unusual word or trip over a carefully crafted line.

Of course, you do have to learn the idiosyncracies of presidents. Nixon, for example, liked the didactic "Now, why do I believe that?" and the much parodied "Let me make it perfectly clear." Ford had problems with the pronunciation of "nuclear," in which he added an extra syllable. One wrote "atomic" instead.

I would also dig into the president's background. I might throw in a reference "to the swallows of Capistrano" for the southern Californian Nixon, or the effect of the "T" formation for former Michigan guard Ford, or a Babe Ruth anecdote for the All-American college first baseman Bush—when he was playing for Yale, Bush was introduced to the dying Home Run legend.

I studded Nixon's speeches with quotations from the statesmen he admired—Woodrow Wilson and Theodore Roosevelt were his favorites. For Ford, whose taste didn't run to biography, I kept to Lincoln and Churchill.

Actually—before Kennedy—quotations were rare in presidential utterances, but in the 1960 campaign Sorensen cited a galaxy of greats to light JFK's path to the presidency—not just the famous in politics but luminaries in poetry and philosophy, too. Sorensen paraded T.S. Eliot, Robert Frost, Ralph Waldo Emerson, and Plato, as well as Jefferson and John Calhoun to convince the voter of young Kennedy's wisdom and knowledge.

I learned early, however, that the esoteric quotation could backfire. In a commencement address I once wrote for Vice President Spiro Agnew, I quoted the French philosopher Albert Camus, "What makes a job a vocation is the service to truth and the service to freedom." Unfortunately, Agnew, unfamiliar with French pronunciation, sounded Camus with an "s." Afterwards, when a reporter asked who "Kamos" was, I explained, "an ancient Greek philosopher."

At a seminar in Harvard, I was asked, "You can't mean, Mr. Humes, that speechwriters are *only* 'cosmeticians' or 'translators'?"

Well, actually there are some occasions when a speechwriter might merit a footnote in history—like Alexander Hamilton's Farewell Address for President Washington. Some others that I can think of are Rick Hendryk's "malaise" speech for President Carter in 1975, Malcolm Moos's draft for President Eisenhower's Farewell Address in 1961, Tony Dolan's work for President Reagan in his address to Parliament in 1981, and Ray Price's "Silent Majority" speech for President Nixon in 1969.

This is what I call, in Plato's words, a "Philosopher-King" speech. Such a talk is not so much a plea for congressional votes as it is an appeal to American values. The president gives to the speechwriter only the most general of guidelines. It is up to the writer to fill in the details. It is every speechwriter's dream to be asked to draft a commencement speech, for he deals with the president directly— not through the filter of a White House chief of staff.

This is the kind of speech that triggers editorials by the *New York Times* or reams of newsprint by columnists.

And then there are those occasions when the speechwriter actually does make policy. I call it "the 3:00 A.M. president." Sometimes— even if the general details of a legislation message have been hammered out—unagreed matters remain because of fights between competing departments. As the various drafts of the proposed message are relayed to various cabinet heads for approval, one cabinet secretary knocks out one word or item and his rival puts it back in. A change goes in—then it's taken out. The beleaguered speechwriter watches the process bounce back and forth as he would a Ping-Pong match. The hours pass from late night into the wee hours of the next day, when the president is scheduled to deliver the message. Finally, the department heads go to bed and the final decision is left to the writer—hence the 3:00 A.M. president.

I remember one message on mass transit by President Nixon. The bone of contention was the funding. Budget Director Arthur Burns demanded it be paid from the gasoline tax, but Secretary of Transportation John Volpe wanted it covered by general revenues. At 3:30, I had to decide. I chose general revenues.

Strangely, my decision drew no backlash. Everyone assumed the president had made the decision. What did draw comment was a line where the Bard in me was trying to transcend "the bureaucratic." I had written, "We shall eliminate the 'mass' in mass transit." I meant the congestion, but at a subcabinet meeting, vetting the talk, Counsel John Ehrlichman said, "What the hell does that mean?" And Budget Director Arthur Burns put down his pipe and surveyed my over two hundred pounds of corporeal splendor and said, "It means that Humes will never be allowed to take a subway or bus again!"

Chapter Two

POLITICAL CHILD

What thing in honour, had my father lost
That need to be revived and breathed in me.
HENRY IV (2)

I am often asked how I ever wound up in the White House drafting speeches for presidents. It all began in 1941 when I was first exposed to that virulent virus that emanates from the swampland known as Foggy Bottom. It's called "Potomac Fever."

Before my family took a trip to Washington that spring, my father, who was a state judge, called up a Harvard Law classmate, a friend of Franklin Roosevelt, and wrangled a letter of introduction to the president.

Daddy parked our brand new Lincoln Zephyr on Pennsylvania Avenue, right in front of the White House, and, armed only with the letter, entered in the hope of meeting the great man. My mother was furious. We were Republicans. As my father left the car, she said, "Sam, you're the leading Republican in our county, and now you're fraternizing with the enemy!" To make her point, my mother dug out a campaign pin saved from the 1940 campaign. It said, "We Don't Want Eleanor Either."

Two hours later my father finally appeared looking sheepish. As my mother glared, he said, "Dear, I know I shouldn't have talked to him. The SOB charmed me!"

In the upscale Vallamont section of Williamsport, there was only one Democratic family—an Episcopalian rector and his wife. Like the Roosevelts, they were patricians who paraded their love for the common man. In 1937, as they attended the wedding of Franklin Delano Roosevelt, Jr., and Ethel DuPont in Wilmington, the clouds opened up. As the cleric later told my father, a reporter had asked the president, "Doesn't the rain somewhat dampen the spirit of the occasion?"

"No" Roosevelt answered. "It's always a grand day when I see so many rich Republicans getting soaked!"

Those two hours in front of the White House that day must have infected me with the Potomac Fever virus. But those most likely to catch Potomac Fever are clearly genetically predisposed. I got from my father a love of history and from my mother a love of the stage.

Actually, my first appearance was attended by all the costuming effects of the stage. On October 31, 1934, my father and mother were invited to a masquerade party by the family obstetrician, Dr. John V. Nutt. The genial doctor, dressed as a Cheshire Cat, greeted my parents at the door. My father, weighing over two hundred pounds, sported two towels as loincloths, along with a feather headdress and red paint befitting an Indian Chief. My mother, a week into her ninth month of pregnancy, appeared as Aunt Jemima in blackface. (It was a half-century before political correctness took over the public domain.)

As she waddled in, my mother said, "Doctor, I'm beginning to feel some twinges."

"Now Elenor, don't ruin my night. First dinner party I've hosted in a year."

At a quarter after eleven, my mother grabbed the doctor's arm. "Hurry call, Dr. Cat," she said.

And off went Aunt Jemima to the Williamsport Hospital driven by the Cheshire Cat with the Indian Chief in hot pursuit. But it was not quite fast enough. On the elevator to the delivery room, I emerged at 11:50 on Halloween night.

Mother was a talented raconteur. Her skills, as well as her bent for mimicry, I either learned or inherited. And my father loved to regale audiences with recitations. After a second-grade recital by me of a Christmas poem, my father said, "Jamie, you're not trying to win a race—slow down and take your time and don't bang down on every rhyme at the end of the line."

When I was only five, my father ran for judge. Campaigning with children was an innovation in 1939. Since he was campaigning at thirty-seven, he would, if elected, be Pennsylvania's youngest judge. Naturally, age was an issue. My father, a prize Latin student in his school days, would quote Tacitus: "Wisdom in a judge is not a matter of age but of temperament."

At one Methodist supper before he spoke, I climbed onto the table and delivered the speech ending with Tacitus, which I lisped, "Tathituth thayth... " My father left the speaking to me that night.

But if temperament includes judgment and wit, Sam Humes was amply qualified. A few months earlier during the Republican primary, his opponent closed his address in a campaign debate with these words:

> I ask all of you on May 5 to vote for
> Charles P. Beidelspacher.

My father rose and said, "On May 5 please vote for Charles P. Beidelspacher," paused, and added, "But on Tuesday, May 6, Election Day, vote for Sam Humes."

My father might not have wanted me to follow him in politics, but he sure wanted to pack some history in his sons' heads. He took us boys to Gettysburg in 1938 for the Seventy-Fifth Reunion of Civil War veterans. What I remember most is a bearded Confederate being pushed in his wheelchair by his former foe.

My father also had me shake hands with the last "daughter of the Revolution." On the Fourth of July in 1942, Judge Humes took his youngest to call on Mrs. Anna Gregory Knight, one hundred years old. My father said, "Jamie, Mrs. Knight's daddy fought in the American Revolution."

In not much more than a cackle, she recited what must have become a litany over the years, "Yes, Grandpappy went down the lane and Pappy followed him saying, 'I want to go, too.' 'All right, Johnny,' said Grandpappy. 'You can be a drummer boy.'"

Years later, I learned that Mrs. Knight was born to John Gregory when he was aged sixty-seven.

On July 4, 1988, I was invited to deliver an address at Independence Hall. I related my visit in 1942 and added, "We claim to be the oldest continuing democracy in the world but think of this—I shook hands with someone whose father fought to forge that democracy."

At the first break of dawn on January 29, 1943, my brother Graham and I were having a pillow fight. Our mother appeared at the door, her face somber.

"Boys," she said. "Your father has gone to heaven."

We sat for breakfast that morning at a table laden with birthday presents for our father. He would have been forty-two on January 29, 1943, if he hadn't died of a cerebral hemorrhage the night before.

Because I was only eight, I think I survived the shock better than my brothers. Samuel, the oldest at twelve, was shattered.

In February 1984, I was walking into the Sterling Hotel in Wilkes-Barre to deliver a speech at a Republican breakfast. A handsome woman in coifed white hair and elegant lavender suit approached me. "Jamie, I'm Jane Muffley. You remember me as Jane Hammer."

The last time I remembered seeing her was at my father's funeral. Jane Hammer, then blonde, had been my father's secretary.

She continued, "Jamie, I've brought your father's desk blotter, engagement book, and a book, *The Autobiography of Benjamin Franklin.*

It was opened to the page of his remarks to the Constitutional Convention in 1787. One sentence was underlined, 'I do not support this Constitution because it is the best but because I am not sure that it is *not* the best.'"

The theme would have permeated his address on citizenship to the PTA of Sheridan School. He never delivered it. He was found slumped in a snow bank next to his car. He had suffered a seizure while attempting to dig himself out.

In 1981, I was a guest on the all-night *Larry King Radio Show* plugging my biography *Churchill—Speaker of the Century*.

About 2:30, a caller from Harrisburg said, "Larry, is your guest any relation to a Judge Sam Humes from Williamsport, Pennsylvania?"

"Yes, he was my father."

"Let me tell you, he was the finest man I ever knew."

Another caller from New Mexico agreed. "That caller from Harrisburg was right—I still have a picture of him on my desk."

An analyst might say that I suffer from a "Jesus Christ syndrome" about my father: the father who dies young is posthumously invested with all the virtues of a saint. My mother sensed that. Years later when I was a typically confused teenager sneaking a look at girlie magazines while entertaining noble aspirations, I was plagued with doubts that I could ever be half the man I had begun to resemble in looks and size.

"Jamie," my mother said, "I remember one night when your father came home. 'Elenor,' he said, 'Let's forget the Firemen's Dinner tonight and have a night in the sack.'"

Though my father, unlike my mother, didn't smoke or drink, he was an earthy man with a zest for life. My mother once told me, "Jamie, your father was the first big man I ever dated. Before I was introduced, someone whispered to me that Sam Humes had been a star lineman for Williams College.

"Well, at that time, I disdained sports. I had just come back from my schoolteacher fellowship at Columbia in New York.

"I said to him, 'I understand you played football at Williams. How interesting.'"

"Your father asked me about Columbia. I said I had studied the American women poets—Emily Dickinson, Sara Teasdale, and Elinor Wylie.

"When he learned I had written a paper on a poem by Elinor Wylie, your father proceeded to recite the whole poem.

"Here," said my mother, "was this big athlete who could quote poetry. He didn't know it but I think he might have taken me to bed that night."

It must have cost my mother a great deal to say this but she wanted to impress on me that my father could give in to all the normal drives of a man—and that he was not Jesus Christ.

My father rarely disciplined me. I remember once I took a cane and imitated Daddy's clerk, Mr. Dooley, who lost his leg in the Spanish-American War. In the sternest tone I had ever heard from him my father said, "James, I never thought I'd see a son of mine making fun of a cripple." I cried all afternoon.

There was another rebuke after his death. One night, in Williamsport, in April 1945, on our street, I heard the sounds of revelry from some of the homes. Someone said, "Roosevelt's dead and we're all celebrating." I came home and said, "Mother, did you hear the good news? Roosevelt is dead!"

My mother flashed her severest schoolmarm glare. "James Calhoun Humes, I am deeply chagrined. We are Republicans, and we did not support Mr. Roosevelt's political policies—but to cheer the president's death—! Your father is looking down from Heaven right now, and he is grievously disappointed in you."

Two years later, aged twelve, I went off to Hill School in Pottstown, Pennsylvania, to join my two brothers—the school my father and grandfather attended. My mother had remarried, unhappily, and we had moved to a farm near Bedford, Pennsylvania.

My father's inscription under his 1919 graduation picture read

"Big in body, mind, and soul." At the Hill, I would gain my six-feet, two-inch height and bearish build. The result was to make me look startlingly like my father.

I also had his retentive mind—what some mistakenly call a photographic memory. (My Latin scores at Hill were the highest ever—except for my father's in 1919.)

Yet, if I had his brains and bulkiness, I didn't inherit his athletic skills. Every teenager wants to be popular but I was obsessive about it. I had to be elected a class officer—just the way my father had been. I analyzed my political prospects. Those who were usually elected were either good in sports or good looking. I was neither.

I put my good memory to work. I mentally filed away the interests, hobbies, and obsessions of those labeled drips and dullards by the "in" crowd. It worked well enough to be elected each year to the Student Committee, which I prized much more than my top grades.

Winning elective office was not the only political spade work I did. Even though I still stuttered and lisped, I tried out for the debate team.

Despite my reverence for General MacArthur, I chose to support Truman's decision to fire the general. To take the Truman side in 1951 was almost treason—at least with my schoolmates.

At Lawrenceville, Choate, and other schools, the preppie audience cheered for our pro-MacArthur opponents, but my partner and I figured the prep school history masters, who would be judging us, would lean our way. Our line was that we revered MacArthur but revered the Constitution more! We also had access to good debate material—my partner "Budgie" Pearre's father was a doctor to, among others, Senator Richard Russell, the then-head of the Senate Armed Services Committee whose staff forwarded us key constitutional points. We received our championship cup.

For a boy who grew up during World War II, heroes on the battlefield were like heroes on the playing field. My favorite subjects in grade school were history and geography.

Listening to Lowell Thomas and his nightly newscast was a ritual at our home. Radio and voice enthralled me. While other Hill boys collected Big Band recordings, I amassed records of orations and poetry.

I had discs of Orson Welles reciting *Macbeth* and *The Ancient Mariner*, and T.S. Eliot reading his *Wasteland*. I also collected famous orations of Abraham Lincoln, Patrick Henry, and Daniel Webster that were delivered by Raymond Massey and other actors.

Later I collected the famous speeches of Churchill and Franklin Roosevelt. I even had some of Theodore Roosevelt and Woodrow Wilson, as well as excerpts from William Jennings Bryan's "Cross of Gold" speech. By age fifteen, I was writing my own Inaugural Address. I would psych myself up first by playing John Sousa marches, and then I would intone in the lowest voice I could muster my presidential words.

Chapter Three

CHURCHILL ACOLYTE

The blessed plot, this earth, this realm, this England.
RICHARD II

T o say Mother was an Anglophile is an understatement. Her high school principal father named her "Nell" in honor of the heroine of *The Old Curiosity Shop*. She was reared on Shakespeare and Charles Dickens, and my parents honeymooned in Britain. We had Dickens china plateware, and our living room coffee table was piled high with copies of *Illustrated London News*, *Punch*, and *Country Life*.

In 1940, my mother would wake me out of a nap to listen to Prime Minister Winston Churchill speak on the radio and afterward question me on what I had learned. Churchill, not Franklin Roosevelt, was our pin-up hero for World War II. We had pictures of him from *Time* and *Illustrated London News*, as well as *Toby* jugs, shortbread tins, and a lead miniature toy soldier bearing his likeness. Churchill even outranked the royal family in my mother's esteem. Her favorite royal was the queen (now the queen mother) who, Mother would remind us, "has no German blood, only Scottish."

My mother identified with Queen Elizabeth because the pregnancy of her first son, Samuel, in 1930, took place at the same time the Princess of York, as she was then called, was carrying what would be her second daughter, Margaret Rose.

In April 1952, I phoned her from Hill School to tell her I had won an English-Speaking Union Scholarship to a British public school. She was exultant! I paid my tribute to my departed mother at the British Embassy when I was inducted into the Order of the British Empire by Queen Elizabeth II in 1994. "Mother, I would never have sailed to England but for you, and I share my pride with you today." By the way, my citation read that I was the only person on either side of the Atlantic to have written biographies of the two greatest Englishmen—Churchill and Shakespeare.

When I boarded the *Queen Mary* with thirty other American prep school scholars, I found a note in her surprise going away gift of cookies: "H.A.V.E. A B.A.L.L." It was an acronym for the seven children of Queen Victoria—Helen, Arthur, Victoria, Edward, Alfred, Beatrice, Alice, Louise, and Leopold—with rhyming ditties reciting the progeny of each.

In consequence, I would amaze my English hosts with my knowledge of royal genealogy. As a father, I would pass on this device to my daughters.

My teachings of Tudors and Stuarts may have led to my daughter Mary's editorship on the *Harvard Crimson*. Later, like Franklin Roosevelt, Theodore White, and Caspar Weinberger, she would head that daily newspaper.

One spring day in 1985, Mary called me and said "Daddy, tonight is the time of 'the turkey shoot,' and forty of our senior staff at the *Crimson* are going to pick one of three of us 'compets' to join the editorial staff."

"I'm one of them, Daddy, but I don't have a chance. They always ask your politics, and if I say I'm Republican or conservative, it's as bad as saying I'm a 'fascist.'"

The next day she called and told me she had been selected.

"Mary," I said, "what did you tell them?"

"Well, Daddy, the first guy got up and said 'I'm a Leninist,' and got cheers."

"The next guy got up and said 'I'm a Castroite'—and there was more applause."

"Then I stood and waited—as you told me to do to get maximal attention—and said, very softly, 'My name is Mary Stuart Humes and I'm a [pause] Monarchist.'"

"Well, Daddy, some in the back must have thought I said 'Marxist' or 'Maoist' or maybe most of them thought 'Monarchist' was really a far-out radical—anyway, I was chosen!"

When I entered Stowe School in September of 1952 to begin my year in England, it was still one of the great country homes of England. I later learned that the exiled Louis XVIII chose Stowe as his exile home and died there.

I was one Yank amongst four hundred British—a figure six feet two, fourteen stones (195 pounds), whose size and accent made me about as inconspicuous as a bear in a ballet.

Warmth of welcome is not the first of English virtues. But in due course I was accepted.

The fall of 1952 was the time General Eisenhower was the Republican candidate for the presidency. It was also the first time British television covered our campaigns. So I had to explain why candidates were sold like soap in jingles for TV advertisements and why live elephants at the Republican convention paraded with the GOP candidate Eisenhower like an ancient Caesar in Rome. They found odd our huge buttons inscribed "I Like Ike" or "I'm Madly for Adlai." "Is that Walt Disney or democracy?" my housemaster Bartram Stephan would ask me.

And come November 1952, I had no one to share my joy in the splendid Republican triumph. In fact, with December holidays near, I had no one with whom to spend the five-week vacation. I dispatched a letter to the hospitality chairman of ESE scholars saying I would like to visit a Scottish castle, a Yorkshire farmer, a member of

Parliament, and a Welsh coal miner. I figured the spread—in class, as well as region—might soften the presumption of the request. Miss Biscoe delivered—well, not the coal miner, but a Methodist parson in the Welsh coal region!

As far as I know, I was the only American boy to put conditions on such invitations. I made sure, however, to pen my thank you notes promptly and send flowers, not only to my hosts, but to Miss Biscoe. After that I could not make a request that was too outlandish.

One thing I didn't ask for was to dance with the queen, but I managed that on my own. A fellow Chandosian—our house was Chandos—said, "Humes, what are you doing around Christmas? If you come to visit us, you might get a peep of the royals."

Nicholas Luddington's father—a retired brigadier—was the steward or manager of Sandringham, one of the royal family's castles. It is from Sandringham that the queen delivers her Christmas Day radio messages.

I arrived on the afternoon of Boxing Day—December 26 is the holiday when traditionally British families would "box up" presents and deliver them to their servants, who had the day off. December 26, 1952, was the sixteenth birthday of Princess Alexandra, and Nicholas had been invited to a small dance in her honor. When the queen's secretary was told that he had an American friend, I was invited too.

For the royal family, the Christmas season of 1952 was a time of muted merriment. King George VI had died the previous February. The twenty-six-year-old Princess Elizabeth immediately became queen, but the coronation was not scheduled until June of 1953. This birthday observance for Alexandra, daughter of the late king's brother, was a private family affair.

An equerry approached me and said, "Mr. Humes, it is appropriate for you to dance with Her Majesty."

For this male adolescent, the queen, decked out in a low-cut gown, was an unnerving display. I resolutely stared at the ceiling as she graciously tried to make me feel at ease. "How do you like England?" "Fine," I shot back monosyllabically.

"How do you find our English Christmas?"

"Fine," I repeated.

And so went the scintillating conversation.

Although I saw Prince Philip on that occasion, I had actually met him before at an ESU function at Dartmouth House off Berkley Square to which my friend, Miss Biscoe, had me invited. Brits, especially the Scots, find the American's love of the tartan droll. When I was introduced to Prince Philip, I said as I had been previously coached, "How do you do, your Royal Highness [afterward we were supposed to say 'sir']." The duke answered, "Why do all you Americans like to proclaim your Scotch background?"

My schoolteacher mother, who was proud of her Graham forebears, had drilled into me that the correct adjective was "Scottish" or "Scots"—not Scotch!

I presumptuously replied, "Sir, as you well know, Scotch is the liquid. My background is Scottish."

Philip chuckled. "Young man, you may well be correct but I venture to say that more Scotch flows in American veins than Scottish."

Although Stowe is relatively recent by British public school standards, it drew almost as many sons of celebrities as Eton.

My house, as I said, was Chandos, and in the 1930s, two Chandosians were Prince Ranier and David Niven, who wrote of his capers there (putting a cow in the chapel) in his autobiography *The Moon Is A Balloon.*

One old Chandosian I particularly remember came back on Old Stoic Day. He found me in my study, which had once been his. We went together to the cricket match with Eton, and while sipping tea between innings, he asked me to visit him one weekend.

"Thank you very much, Mr. Milne."

"No," he said, "call me Christopher." His full name was Christopher Robin Milne.

At his house one evening, he said, "Take the bear up with you. Someday you will want to tell your children that you hugged the original Winnie-the-Pooh."

His playwright father had created him in his children's books in 1924. He was named after Winston Churchill ("Pooh" was young Milne's baby-talk name for bear).

A. A. Milne, like many British fathers, did not communicate easily with his children. His Christopher Robin books were an attempt to surmount that, although for the son it would be an embarrassment in school, and later in the RAF in which he served in World War II. (It is noteworthy that two great leaders, Teddy Roosevelt and Winston Churchill, would both generate ursine cults.)

I got to meet Churchill himself on May 29. It was at the Commonwealth Parliamentary Association banquet, a gala event at which the heads of government in the British Commonwealth of Nations assemble in London, under the ceremonial aegis of the queen.

Through my British fairy godmother, Miss Biscoe, I was invited to one of the receptions. Martin Gilbert, in his eight-volume epic biography of Churchill, describes my meeting.

> As the Coronation approached, Churchill's mind
> turned toward earlier Queens, Elizabeth and Anne,
> whom he had written about, and Victoria, whom he had
> served. At the Commonwealth Parliamentary Association
> Banquet, he told James C. Humes, an eighteen-year-old
> English-speaking Union Scholar at Stowe,
> "Young man, study, study history. In history lie all the
> secrets of statecraft."

The terse account does not describe the impact the meeting had on me. Since then, I have met everyone who has occupied the White House from Eisenhower to Bush, but when I shook hands with Churchill, I knew I was meeting the greatest man in the world!

To shake hands with Churchill was like meeting Napoleon or Julius Caesar except that Churchill represented not authoritarian principles, but the ideals of freedom and democracy. The moment left me giddy, and I went back to Stowe that night and took down my photo of Ted Williams and put up one of Churchill. It was a rite of passage—youth to manhood. History would supplant baseball as my avocation, and politics would become my vocation.

Chapter Four

IKE IDOLATER

He is a soldier fit to stand by Caesar.
OTHELLO

he first time I met President Eisenhower was not auspicious. As a Young Republican of the District of Columbia chapter, I was put on the Host Committee for a $500-a-seat gala in June 1956, staged by the Republican National Committee. For me, it was a "freebie." All I had to do was usher VIPs to their respective tables. After the festivities had started, we Young Republicans would ourselves find seats that the fat cats had paid for but hadn't shown up for.

The dinner was held at the Uline Arena—an ice hockey rink converted for the occasion to a mammoth banquet hall for a presidential talk to Republican contributors. One of the Secret Service spotted my host badge and asked, "Where's the men's room—the president has to relieve himself." I quickly gathered that Eisenhower, who was recovering from a bout with ileitis, had a weak bladder.

But I didn't know where the men's room was. Was it at the north end of the arena, or was that the ladies room? I pointed north and ran ahead to scout the situation. Alas, it was the ladies room! What

31

was I to do? I couldn't have the president retrace his steps and go all around to the south side.

I knocked at the door and in stentorian tones announced "Emergency—President of the United States. Everybody out. Everybody out!"

Two middle-aged matrons burst out like pheasants flushed from the wood brush. As the president approached, I flung the door of the restroom open and turned it to the wall to hide the telltale sign.

President Eisenhower, with two Secret Service men trailing him, entered, and I closed the door. When I could hear that the pressing business was finished, I opened it.

The president must have noted the unfamiliar accoutrements, for, as he exited, he frowned and drilled me with his electric blue eyes.

I HAD LEFT WILLIAMS COLLEGE for Washington, D.C., in search of political adventure. For someone who had met Winston Churchill and danced with the queen, campus life in the remote Berkshires seemed detached from the real world.

But while there, I was active in the Williams Young Republicans. As a moderate Republican, I organized a trip to the University of Massachusetts to hear Senator Joe McCarthy, at which, instead of booing, we laughed. I later met the senator at a party at Senator Hennings house in Washington (I was dating his daughter, Sue) and found him not so much a bogeyman as a likable buffoon. My quarrel with "Tail Gunner" Joe was that the Reds in government benefitted by his recklessness.

At Williams, I also babysat for Professor James McGregor Burns, the noted political scientist who authored *The Lion and the Fox*, a biography of Franklin Roosevelt. Burns was also president of the Massachusetts ADA (Americans for Democratic Action).

One night I was looking after the children in Williamstown, while Burns and his wife journeyed to Boston. Professor Burns was introducing the newly elected Senator John Kennedy as the ADA's featured speaker. Kennedy, to Burns' embarrassment, asked the group to disband because of its "soft on communism" policies. (It should be remembered that Congressman John Kennedy had secretly contributed to Dick Nixon in his Senate race against Helen Gahagan Douglas in 1950.) A miffed James Burns told me, "Jamie, Jack really would be a liberal if his father let him."

(Ivy League colleges in the 1950s were light years away from the way they were in the 1960s. When I returned to speak to Williams in a seminar in 1967, the four P's—Pills, Pot, Politics, and Pop Music—had transformed preppies into protestors.)

Unlike most of my Williams classmates, I was a political activist. At the time, I convinced myself that what was happening in Washington was more important than what was happening in Williamstown. But in retrospect, I think it was a cop-out. I was rebelling against the discipline and demands of college.

I quit Williams to join the Marines. The physical exam revealed I had a high blood pressure problem. Instead of returning to Williams, I stayed at the farm in Bedford with my dispirited mother, who would eventually take her own life.

When my stepfather remarried three months later, I had already exited to Washington, lusting for the world of politics. Of course, I didn't call it that. I pontificated about "a sense of purpose."

I know that age makes rosy the impressions of youth, but today's senators make their predecessors in the 1950s seem like titans. The 1990s variety seem like clones of blow-dried TV anchormen. Dan Quayle, whom the media reviled, is not all that much different from the Al Gores and John Kerrys and Max Baucuses of today.

In the 1950s, the senators seemed like indigenous trees that grow out of their native clime and habitat. Whatever you thought of their politics, the courtly drawl of a Senator Russell from Georgia, the patrician tones of a Leverett Saltonstall from Massachusetts, the lower East Side accent of a New Yorker like Jacob Javits, not to mention the drawl of a Lyndon Johnson from Texas or the bass rumble of an Everett Dirksen from Illinois, offered views as divergent as their accents. Their speeches on the floor imparted texture and character, unhomogenized by TV media demands for smooth looks and glib statements.

Today, politicians—with the singular exceptions of some like Pat Moynihan, Alan Simpson, Sam Nunn, Fritz Hollings, and Jesse Helms—change their views as they would their ties to fit the latest fashion. They read remarks drafted by speechwriters, filtered by pollsters, and edited by media consultants.

Whatever their political differences, neither President Truman nor President Eisenhower fit this mold. I met former President Truman in the Capitol in April 1960.

Because my wife was working full-time for Vice President Nixon (and I, part-time), I was allowed to take an English visitor into the Senate Dining Room. He was Edward Moulton-Barrett (a great-nephew of poet Elizabeth Barrett-Browning), who was a leader of the British Liberal Party. I had stayed several times with the Barretts during my year in England.

At the next table, I observed the former president lunching with Missouri Senator Stuart Symington, whom he was promoting for the White House to stop Jack Kennedy. While they were having dessert and coffee, I approached the table and said, "Mr. President, I have with me an Englishman who thinks your leadership on the Marshall Plan and NATO made the difference in preserving a free Europe. Although I'm a Republican, I think your resolve inspires those like myself who are considering politics."

Truman answered in words not unlike Churchill's advice. "Young man, my advice is to read American history and tell the truth. You Republicans say, 'I always give 'em Hell,' but I only tell the truth and you Republicans thought it was Hell."

Truman, of course, deserves credit for his anticommunist foreign policy initiatives such as NATO, the Marshall Plan, and the Truman

Doctrine. Yet, when Churchill spoke at his invitation at Westminster College in Fulton, Missouri, in 1946, Truman disassociated himself from Churchill's Iron Curtain warning. In fact, on his instructions, his secretary of state, Dean Acheson, snubbed Churchill by not showing up at a diplomatic reception for him a day later. Even worse, recently released classified files reveal that Truman invited Stalin to come to Missouri and give his side of the story and offered to send the Battleship *Missouri* to pick him up. That story, reported in the *Washington Post* in April 1996, has been omitted by his biographers. Some of them, like Merle Smith, relied on his fictionally embroidered reminiscences in 1953 after he had left office. His remembered tongue-lashing of General MacArthur at Wake Island, for example, never happened.

Another incident that did happen in those conversations after he left the White House was told to me by David Susskind. (He was filming me in my one-man Churchill show.) Susskind said that each morning, in preparation for a show, he would arrive at Truman's house at Independence. He would wait on the porch on a cold February day while Mrs. Truman went to inform her husband of his arrival. After about the fourth morning, he asked the president in his walk why he was never asked inside.

"You're a Jew, David, and no Jew has ever been in the house."

A nonplussed Susskind replied, "I am amazed that you who recognized Israel and championed the integration of the army would say such a thing!"

"David," he explained, "this is not the White House—it's the Wallace house. Bess runs it, and there's never been a Jew inside the house in her or her mother's lifetime."

This has been confirmed by Eddie Jacobs, Truman's former partner in the failed haberdashery, who said that he was never invited inside the house.

Truman had told the blunt truth. Years later I heard his daughter talk about her father's penchant for blunt talk. A beau came to visit her at the White House. President Truman took him to the Rose

Garden. "You see these roses? Best damn roses you've ever seen. You know why? Fresh manure. You want to have a good garden, you've got to have manure."

Margaret later told her mother, "Don't you think Daddy could say 'fertilizer' instead of 'manure'?"

Bess Truman replied, "Margaret, do you know how many years it took me to get him to say 'manure'?"

At a dinner party in New York in late 1973, when Watergate was beginning to emerge, the guests tried to draw out Margaret Truman's views on the subject.

Margaret Truman, to her credit, said, "Everyone knows I'm no supporter of Nixon, but in my years in the White House I promised myself never to criticize the incumbent president because I've seen what it's like to be on the inside and the target of the press."

Her husband, *New York Times* editor Clifton Daniels, interposed, gesturing with the polished fingernails of his hand.

"Come on, Margaret, you've said Nixon was as guilty as sin."

Margaret replied sharply, "What I said in the privacy of the bedroom I didn't intend to be repeated publicly."

Harry Truman had no use for the man who succeeded him. On the drive to the Capitol on Inauguration Day in 1953, the outgoing Truman's exchange of words with General Eisenhower was brief and brusque—and the feeling was reciprocated.

When President Truman—after Eisenhower's victory in November—recalled the general's son, John, from Korea for active duty in the White House, he angered Eisenhower, who thought Truman had done it to make it look as if the newly elected president had pulled strings for his son.

Actually, in the case of Truman, the enmity for Eisenhower was not only political put personal. It had all the animus of a spurned suitor. During World War II, Truman's admiration for the Kansas-bred soldier verged on hero-worship. There had been a connection between the Truman and Eisenhower families—Truman's brother

Vivian had shared a boarding house room with Ike's brother Arthur. It was only natural that former Captain Truman out of a Kansas City National Guard would cheer the rise of Eisenhower who jumped quickly from colonel to supreme commander.

President Truman would indirectly sound out General Eisenhower for the vice presidency in 1948 and, then, in 1952, Truman wanted him to be the Democratic presidential nominee. Instead, Eisenhower accepted the Republican nomination and ran to "clean up the mess in Washington." That charge rankled Truman.

The press often painted Eisenhower as having a brighter personality than intellect. The perception is far from the truth. Anyone who worked under Eisenhower found him quick in mind and cold in manner. As a staffer under Eisenhower told me, "You quickly find out that he's the general and you're the private and he and you know the difference."

Ike's son, John, confirmed this. He told me that in his 6:00 A.M. briefings, his father was curt and brusque. He would nod or ask pointed questions. He would offer no small talk about health, politics, or grandchildren.

In late 1960, following the Nixon defeat by Kennedy, I did part-time speechwriting. Most of the chief writers in the White House were out lining up job interviews.

I took something into the outgoing President Eisenhower. He slammed his glassed to the desk and said, "What's the QED?"

"QED, sir?" I asked—I wasn't associating geometry with the general.

"QED," he answered, "QUOD ERAT DEMONSTRANDUM. What's the bottom line? What's the message? What do you want the audience to do when the speech is over? And another thing…"

Just then an aide popped in. A meeting with the Little League World Series co-captains.

As if he had pushed a magic button somewhere on his coat, the five-star general transformed into Ike.

"Boys," he said, "did you ever go skinny-dipping?"

They nodded.

"Back in Kansas," Eisenhower continued, "these two boys were drying themselves in the sun. The light-haired lad asked his dark-haired friend, 'What would you like to be if you could be anything in the world?' The boy answered, 'President of the United States,' and then asked his companion, 'What would like to be if you could be anything in the world?' and he replied, 'Pitcher for the New York Giants.'"

"Well, that's America," said Ike. "You can have any dream. Maybe you won't make it. The boy who wanted to be president became president all right—president of an Abilene dairy and creamery. As for the boy who wanted to be that Giant pitcher, he failed too. That was me!"

When General Eisenhower turned his face to the public, he became Ike—a grown-up Huck Finn, as portrayed by Norman Rockwell.

The beaming smile of Eisenhower could light up a dark room. With his bald, shiny pate that topped a ruddy complexion, his visage was almost that of a haloed saint painted by a fifteenth-century Italian.

After my dressing down by Eisenhower, I beat a retreat from the Oval Office and went to Fred Fox, the pastor-turned-speechwriter. (At Williams, I taught Sunday School at his Williamstown Congregational Church.) Reverend Fred Fox quoted the dictates of Eisenhower, who once drafted speeches for General MacArthur in the Philippines: "If you can't put the bottom-line message on the inside of a matchbook, you're not doing your job."

Eisenhower, by the way, had this comment on MacArthur. "Mac suffered from an 'eye' problem." I thought he meant maybe glaucoma or a detached retina. Then he added, "He was addicted to the perpendicular pronoun."

In 1966, prompted by his son John in my presence, General Eisenhower repeated his list of the five greatest men he had ever known.

Churchill and de Gaulle made it. FDR did not. John Foster Dulles made the grade. "Foster," explained Eisenhower, "was born to diplomacy. His grandfather and uncle were secretaries of state. He attended the Hague Conference in 1912 and the Versailles Conference in 1917. With the exception of one, Foster knew all about the players in world politics."

"Who was that?" I asked.

"Myself." Eisenhower was modest, but not falsely modest!

Two others on his all-time list made it for restraint of ego. One, of course, was George Marshal, his greatest hero. The other was a surprise—British General Charles "Peter" Portal, because, when an Allied decision had to be made that seemed to favor the Americans, Portal would take the brunt of it by insisting it was his idea.

Not the least reason that Eisenhower was jumped over a hundred officers senior to him to be head of the Allied armies in 1942 was this facade of modest affability.

In the spring of 1967, the ex-president received, at his home in Gettysburg, General Harold Johnson, who was then the head of the Freedom Foundation at Valley Forge. The subject of press coverage of the Vietnam War came up. General Johnson, who once had been chairman of the Joint Chiefs of Staff, said, "Herodotus wrote about the Peloponnesian War that one cannot be an armchair general twenty miles from the front."

Eisenhower nodded, repeating his guest's words, "Herodotus… the Peloponnesian War." Afterward, I, an indefatigable collector of quotations, asked the exact wording of the Herodotus quotation.

Eisenhower, whom the pro–Adlai Stevenson press characterized as unlettered, replied, "First, it wasn't Herodotus, but Aemilius Paulanus. Second, it was the not the Peloponnesian War, but the Punic War with Carthage. And third, he misquoted."

When I asked why he hadn't corrected the general he answered, "I got where I did by knowing how to hide my ego and hide my intelligence. I knew the actual quote, but why should I embarrass him?"

Yet the impression of the bumbling Ike persists. His garbled syntax at press conferences might have reinforced that image. Yet on one occasion it was deliberate.

When a reporter asked the president whether the NATO armies had the authority to discharge nuclear missiles from the field, Eisenhower gave a reply that would have made Casey Stengel sound lucid. Often, it seemed as if the subject in his labyrinthine sentences wouldn't be able to find the predicate in a thousand years with radar.

Afterward, Jim Haggerty, the press secretary, asked Eisenhower what was the real policy. He answered, "If I told them they had the authority, it would scare the hell out of our allies. If I said they didn't, I'd be taking away their quick retaliatory power."

I heard Joe Califano tell of the time in 1965 he was sent up by President Johnson to brief Eisenhower on the Vietnam situation. Califano said, "Mr. President, I understand you just want me to go through the motions of listening and noting carefully what the general says."

"Joe," drawled Johnson, "did you believe all that crap the reporters and we Democrats said about Eisenhower? I want you to put down in your notes every sigh, every frown, every time he rolls his eyes or looks to the sky—he's a wise old man."

Even Republicans tended to forget that the aging ex-president was still on top of military matters. At a National Republican Council meeting in 1965—a Republican National Committee group composed of men like Nixon, Dewey, and former Secretary of Defense Tom Gates—I was privileged to attend as a sergeant of arms to relay phone messages that came from the outside.

The group had assembled to hear recommendations from study groups and then issue a statement under the former president's name. One congressman delivered a report that President Johnson was emasculating NATO with his cuts. All were nodding until they saw Eisenhower stabbing his yellow pad with his pencil.

"Congressman," he interrupted, "who gave you these figures?"

"General, he's a three-star general…"

"Don't count stars with me congressman. I put them there." Then he added, "Congressman, generals lie!" And he proceeded to go over all the force and military hardware numbers in question without notes.

Historians have labeled Eisenhower a do-nothing president. Well, if not running up deficits or waging foreign wars is doing nothing, he makes idleness a presidential ideal.

Liberals counter by charging that his domestic achievements were a blank slate except for a national highway program drafted for the new suburbanites. They forget that Eisenhower signed the first two civil rights bills ever enacted—two more than President Kennedy.

Eisenhower shattered the stereotype that generals are ill-prepared to be president. Before he took his oath of office, scribes widely quoted President Truman's dig that "Ike will find that as president you can't just give an order and expect it to be done." David Eisenhower, Ike's grandson, rightly points out that General Eisenhower had more staff answerable to him in London in 1944 than all the government employees in the nation under Roosevelt in 1933. Eisenhower in London was arranging concordats with kings, negotiating with heads of state, and, at the same time, planning and supervising the greatest deployment of forces in history—the Normandy invasion.

Chapter Five

KENNEDY CRITIC

O, what a noble mind is here o'er thrown,
The courtier's soldier's scholar's eye tongue sword
The expectancy and rose of the fair state
The glass of fashion and the mould of form
HAMLET

T he first encounter I had with John Kennedy is one that I now regret. In May of 1960, my wife and I went one Sunday night to a movie theater in Georgetown to see a double feature of Alec Guinness—*Man in the White Suit* and *The Lavender Hill Mob.*

After the first showing, a couple settled to the right of me and my wife. My ears perked up when I heard a Boston-accented voice saying, "Alec Guinness is the funniest actor…"

I looked over to find the soon-to-be nominated-for-president John Kennedy two seats away from me on the aisle. Next to him was a blonde young companion who did not look like Jackie.

At the time, both my wife and I were working for Vice President Nixon, who, because of the recent dropout of Governor Rockefeller, had no opposition for the Republican nomination. Flouting all precepts of gentlemanly behavior, my eyes strayed to survey the geographical position of Senator Kennedy's hands during *The Lavender Hill Mob.*

When the movie ended, we rose to leave. The senator was awaiting the theater's second showing. My wife exited, with me following. Quite by accident, I tripped over Kennedy's crossed leg that jutted in my path.

With the Harvard soft "r" he said, "I'm sorry about that." I replied in stentorian tones that shook the theater, "THAT'S QUITE ALL RIGHT, SENATOR KENNEDY!"

I was quite a partisan in the 1960 presidential election. Although I was a full-time student at law school, I managed to make a lot of campaign speeches back in Pennsylvania. My brother Graham rented a sound truck. With march music blaring, we would drive through Philadelphia and find a stop for a makeshift rally. Each of us would mount the back platform of the open truck and then deliver the raw meat of political attack to the gathering crowds.

In the heart of ghetto Philadelphia, we were sometime joined by Cecil Moore, Pennsylvania's equivalent of New York's celebrated Adam Clayton Powell. Moore, however, had honed his oratory not from preaching, but from pleading in his criminal defense work. Moore would rip into John Kennedy's weak civil rights record and his cozy relationship with the South, saying, "His only experience with colored folk are those he tips at the country club and screws in Havana whorehouses."

To one heckler who baited Moore with curses, the street-smart lawyer answered, "What's the matter, your father was a bachelor?"

To a white man who challenged his description of conditions for the blacks, he returned, "Now, you just put your head in a bucket of Man-Tan and see if it ain't true."

Two of the applause lines I remember delivering on the back of that sound truck were these:

> When John Kennedy is attacked for dodging civil
> rights issues, they answer that "he is a man of enormous
> principle."

> Well, he has principal, enough 'principal'—to buy the
> White House.

The other had to do with Senator Kennedy saying that the islands off Taiwan weren't worth defending.

> We know that Dick Nixon will never give an island
> or an inch to Red China or anybody. From Caracas to
> the Kremlin, Dick Nixon has stood up to communism.

Another blot in the Kennedy foreign policy record was his telegram to Eisenhower after the U2 incident in Russia insisting that the president should apologize to Khrushchev.

In October, Bobby Kennedy came to downtown Philadelphia to address a packed crowd of thousands in front of City Hall. Somehow, I managed with false identification to get to the speaker's rostrum by sidling and nudging my way to the front microphone.

Just as Kennedy rose to speak, I grabbed the microphone and yelled, "Are you going to apologize to Khrushchev, too?" I was quickly ushered away by police.

At a television-covered debate at the University of Pennsylvania, my opponent was an earnest young Democrat who brought notes on three-by-five cards carefully stacked and labeled by subject.

Just as he was to begin his opening presentation, I slipped him a note, which read, "Bob, your fly is undone."

It wasn't, but it rattled him as he tried to steal looks at his zipper.

The toughest audience was a group of Jewish senior citizens. My Democratic opponent, a state legislator, was Jewish and almost sixty.

I knew I had a tough sell. First, I flipped through my cross-quote file. "Cross-quotesmanship" is the term I coined to describe the stratagem of citing liberals to advance a conservative objective, or vice versa. To quote a Barry Goldwater attack on Kennedy's qualifications to be president is hardly as persuasive as saying, "Former Secretary of

State Dean Acheson once said, "The senator's grasp of foreign affairs is limited." For a Jewish audience, I liked quoting Eleanor Roosevelt on JFK's ducking a vote to censure Senator Joseph McCarthy: "Kennedy has written a book entitled *Profiles in Courage*. Well, he ought to display a little less profile and a little more courage."

I had been told previously that the audience particularly wanted to hear Nixon's position on Medicare legislation. I called a friend in Senator Javits's office, developed from my days with his friend and colleague, Ken Keating. Vice President Nixon had endorsed Javits's bill.

> When John Kennedy attacks Nixon on Medicare, he
> is slandering the great American Jacob Javits. The Nixon
> program is the Javits program. And for Kennedy to
> imply that Jake Javits is insensitive to the needs of senior
> citizens...

But it was my closing that brought my Democratic opponent to his feet with fists clenched.

> I think Eleanor Roosevelt was right again that "you
> cannot ignore the record of Joseph Kennedy in assessing
> the character of his son."
> It was Joe Kennedy who praised Hitler and said he
> was a responsible German nationalist.
> It was Joe Kennedy who said Britain should surren-
> der in 1940.
> And it's Joe Kennedy who's buying the election for
> his son today.
> So I ask you to bear in mind the sacred words of the
> Talmud:
> As the tree is bent, so grows the twig.

Three years later, after I had delivered a eulogy for the slain

Kennedy in the State House of Pennsylvania, Eddie Moore, the eighty-four-year-old House parliamentarian, wrote a note to me saying, "Yours was the finest speech I have heard in my forty years in the House." If that was true, the explanation owes more to the occasion than my oratory. The last assassination was that of McKinley in 1901. It would be strange if the eulogy of a murdered president didn't trigger a greater emotional reaction than a speech on highways or schools.

Still, I did follow my cardinal rule in public speaking: tailor it to the audience. That House chamber was full of professional politicians, all of whom liked to think they were daily exposing themselves to censure and criticism for a public service that made so many demands for so little pay.

I quoted the Letter of Peter in the Bible: "Walk worthy in the vocation in which ye are called." Then I added:

> John Kennedy walked worthy in his vocation. You
> on that side of the aisle saw him as a gallant champion
> —we saw him as a worthy foe. If politics or public ser-
> vice requires sacrifice, John Kennedy made the ultimate
> sacrifice.

After some more paeans to the late president, I closed with the words:

> In the rocks of Thermopylae one Greek carved out
> his epitaph before he died in that heroic struggle against
> the Persians. "Go stranger and to Sparta tell that we in
> faithful public service fell."
> Fellow members, John Kennedy fell in public service
> but his sacrifice has ennobled our profession of politics.

There is no doubt that because of Kennedy many idealistic

students would choose government as a career. Kennedy had taken the image of politics out of smoke-filled rooms. Politics had become public service.

But, that said, the record of Kennedy was mostly rhetorical. If you are a liberal, your real hero should be Lyndon Johnson, who accomplished in three months what Kennedy had only talked about in three years. Kennedy's most substantive legislation was a tax cut to which Jack Kemp has never tired of pointing. But then, lowering taxes in 1962 was about as hard as passing a resolution on motherhood.

Indeed, I argued at a seminar at Williams College in 1982 that the record (not the rhetoric) of Richard Nixon was more progressive than that of John Kennedy. Rapprochement with China, the establishment of the EPA (the Environmental Protection Agency), the Philadelphia plan for minority hiring, the eighteen-year-old vote, and the huge subsidies for arts and cancer research are all proof of that. And that doesn't even count supporting the Moynihan negative income tax for the poor that the Democrats opposed as too radical!

The "martyr" death of Kennedy embalmed his moment in history. Never would it be subjected to the test and accountability of time.

Kennedy fans speak wistfully of Camelot, but the substance of the Hollywood pasteboard sets fabricated for the musical of that name is missing. Not on view were Kennedy's liaisons with Judith Exner, the Mafioso moll, and many, many others, or his administration's wiretapping of Martin Luther King, Jr.

For that reason, I always felt some sympathy for Lyndon Johnson, who would be compared not to the performance of Kennedy, but to his promises. From the vantage point of a staffer on Capitol Hill, Johnson had been a giant in the 1950s. As a political animal, he was a specimen the likes of which will never be seen again. At six feet, three inches, his swaggering presence radiated power like the scent of perfume on Zsa Zsa Gabor. The first time I really met Lyndon

Johnson was at a reception in the Senate caucus room. I was then working for Ken Keating of New York.

LBJ squinted down at me and drawled, "Humes, is that your name? Come over and have some 'horse doves' with me."

At that time, I thought he didn't know the French pronunciation of "hors d'oeuvres," but in retrospect, he was just pulling the chain of this preppie-dressed easterner.

"Are you the guy," he said as he bent down to straighten my tie, "that was described in that article the other day as brilliant?"

"Yes, sir, but I'm not brilliant."

"You know what I would do if you worked on my staff? I'd fire you," he drawled. "Every time I see some aide described as brilliant, I know he's been leakin' to the press—and you're leakin' all over like an unweaned puppy dog."

LBJ was as shrewd as he was crude. On an IQ test, I bet he would have scored higher than John Kennedy. He hadn't the gloss of Choate and Harvard but in sharpness of mind and quickness to cut to the core of a problem, he had few peers.

But on one occasion, I was at hand when he wrongly sized up the situation. At the airport, as the vice president was leaving for his tour of Latin America in 1958, he was asked by a reporter what he thought of the significance of the trip.

"Pure chicken shit," he said.

When Nixon made his triumphant return weeks later after braving communist mobs in Caracas, the first to greet him when he stepped off the plane was the Senate majority leader, saying, "Welcome home, Dick."

Afterward, LBJ was asked by the same journalist, "Senator, didn't you liken the vice president's trip to poultry excrement?"

LBJ drawled, "What you in the press don't understand is how sometimes 'chicken shit' can overnight become 'chicken salad'."

Senator Keating once sneaked in this jibe at LBJ. Johnson had just emerged from Walter Reed Hospital where he had tests, in pursuance of any race for the presidency in 1960. (He had suffered a heart attack in 1956.)

Keating approaching Johnson in the Senate corridor and said:

"Lyndon, how's the cholesterol count?"

"Well, fine, Ken," answered Johnson uncertainly.

Keating then asked, "How's the albumen?"

"Fine, Ken, but… "

"And Lyndon," continued Keating, "how's your urine?"

"Why do you ask, Ken?"

"Well," replied Keating, "I want to make sure that the stuff you're throwing our way in the Senate is 100 percent pure."

Vice President Nixon liked Kennedy but respected Johnson. He had gotten to know Kennedy in his House days. At a party at the vice president's home in 1959, Nixon told me that the only ticket that could beat him in 1960 was a combination of Kennedy and Johnson.

"Jamie, the press would have you believe that Rockefeller appeals more to Democrats. Actually, polls show I do, but the Democrats I appeal to are Catholics from the North and Protestants from the South. That's why a ticket of Kennedy and Johnson would be tough."

"But they'd never get together."

"Wait and see," was his prophetic response.

Ken Keating once told me the Johnson secret of his domination of the Senate.

Johnson confided to him, "I just imagine what this or that senator thinks about when he is shaving in the morning. Is it a highway for a city in his state? Is it a judgeship for his nephew? I make it my business to know those kind of things, and then I own him."

Keating, by the way, would be central casting's conception of a senator—white-maned, ruddy-faced, with a twinkle in his eye. (He would lose reelection against Robert Kennedy in the Democratic landslide of 1964, mainly due to the outpouring of sympathy for the Kennedy family after JFK's assassination.)

Keating taught me a lot about politics. As congressman, he was in spending a conservative, in civil rights a liberal, and in foreign policy an outspoken anticommunist. (In 1962, he was ridiculed by President Kennedy, at first, when he correctly assessed the Soviet buildup in Cuba.)

Once, when I asked him why his civil rights records didn't win more black votes, Keating explained, "I don't expect black votes."

"No—but it's the Jewish vote I'm going after."

Another insight he passed on to me was this: "Most voters are conservative generally, but liberal specifically." In other words, they are conservative except when it comes to programs that apply to them. That's why he liked his speeches to ring with references to "flag, family, and God."

When "In God We Trust" was only on coins, he pushed to have it on the dollar. He was a master at dreaming up uncontroversial resolutions that would get press ink. Once he even proposed that Franklin Roosevelt, as well as Dwight Eisenhower, be added to Mount Rushmore.

A moderate New York Republican, Keating was often likened to his Pennsylvania neighbor, Hugh Scott, who was also elected to the Senate in 1958 after many terms in the House.

Hugh Scott was an urbane, mustached, native Virginian, whose first passion was collecting Oriental jade. I once described Scott to a Philadelphia magazine: "Hugh Scott is the only senator who would be comfortable in Medicean Florence. He could spend all morning plotting how to poison his brother-in-law and all afternoon reviewing his objets d'art."

His administrative assistant called me to protest my characterization, but Scott himself later told me he rather liked it.

Scott was a WASP and FFV (First Family of Virginia) whose collateral ancestor was Zachary Taylor. (I once gave him for his birthday a letter signed by the fourteenth president.) Yet he was a wizard in crafting ethnic support.

He joined the Pennsylvania Sons of Italy, claiming his ancestor was Grotius Scotti, although his paternal name clearly suggests British antecedents.

In 1964, in the year of the Goldwater debacle that would swamp Keating, Scott fired off a telegram to Acting Attorney-General Katzenbach, requesting an investigation of an Arab assassination plot against him.

Walter Annenberg, staunch Republican and publisher of the Philadelphia *Inquirer*, who was never inhibited by the facts, printed this headline four days before the election "ARAB ASSASSINATION PLOT AGAINST SCOTT."

Scott won the election by a few thousand votes against a popular Democrat, Genevieve Blatt. It was "a profile of courage" for Hugh Scott—he stood up against every Arab vote in Pennsylvania—all two of them.

In 1962, Scott blocked the Old Guard's candidate, Judge Woodside, by pushing Bill Scranton for governor. Yet Scranton did not trust him.

Once, I asked what exactly a certain gubernatorial aide, Bill Murphy, did for him.

Scranton laughed, and said, "Murphy? He's Hugh Scott's spy."

Nixon also took a wary view of the wily Pennsylvanian. I was in his New York law office in 1963, and I told him that on a certain matter I had a commitment from Hugh Scott.

Nixon arched his eye and said, "Was it written out? Do you have a copy? Was it notarized?"

In 1960, the Senate was the central scenario in the filming of Allen Drury's bestselling novel *Advise and Consent*. If you've seen the movie that starred Charles Laughton and Walter Pigeon, you'll remember that one senator is always pictured asleep in his chair. Actually, he was the only actual senator in the film. Henry Ashurst was a Democrat from New Mexico, who served in the period during and after World War I—before the days of rich pension plans. Carl Hayden, the eighty-eight-year-old pro-tem of the Senate, persuaded the film company to put his former colleague from New Mexico in the film. I met Ashurst, an aged man who left his retirement home for this appearance for which he would be generously compensated.

Ashurst told me how, as a Woodrow Wilson supporter, he had announced for the League of Nations and then because of pressure back home changed. He gave this reason for the switch in a speech to his colleagues: "There are occasions when every man must rise above principle."

Chapter Six

POLITCAL 'WANNA-BE'

I'll play the orator as well as Nestor,
Deceive more slyly than Ulysses could
And, like a Sinon, take another Troy.
I can add colours to the chameleon,
Change shapes with Proteus for advantage,
And set the murderous Machiavel to school.
HENRY VI, PART III

A t 12:01 P.M., January 21, 1961, when John Fitzgerald Kennedy was sworn in as the thirty-fourth president of the United States, I was in Room 360 of the Senate Office Building (now the Russell Building) packing up the belongings of Richard Nixon. Nixon, as outgoing vice president, was one of the bit players in the inaugural ceremonies. My wife and I arrived to begin the weary job of sorting and packing the files. A deep snow, falling since early morning, had clogged the roadways. Our apartment, catercorner from the Old House Office Building, made it possible for us to take a snowless, subterranean route, dry and warm, from the Cannon Building at 1st and C Streets, Southeast, to the Capitol and then to the Senate Office Building.

At Nixon's office (as vice president of the Senate, it was his chief office) we had to step across a few drunken celebrants who were sleeping it off outside Room 359, the office of Senator John Kennedy. It was an irony in the 1960 campaign that the nerve centers of the two presidential candidacies were only a few feet apart. (At that time, vice presidents did not have offices in the White House.)

I was not paid in cash for my volunteer efforts, but received instead something far more valuable. Nixon gave me a letter Winston Churchill had sent him congratulating him for an address to The Pilgrims.[3]

The Nixon defeat was not a surprise. On the weekend before election day, our own polls showed us a bit behind, but the momentum was with us. It was going to be razor close, and so it was.

Actually, the only bet I wagered on the election, I won. I had bet my law school classmate, Chuck Manatt (the future Democratic national chairman), that Nixon would carry California.

Still, no presidential campaign ever gripped me more—perhaps because it was the first.

There was the shock when we Nixon staffers alit from our chartered plane to Chicago to learn that the Boss had capitulated to Rockefeller's demands for the platform in return for the governor's endorsement.

There was the excitement of Walter Judd's keynote speech with his litany of rhetorical questions. ("Was it the Republican administration who lost China? Was it the Republican administration who gave away Eastern Europe in Yalta?" Thirty years later, Dr. Judd told me that just before he was to mount the podium, he changed all the charges from the declarative to the interrogative.)

There was the frustration of the Nixon campaign with the media. When Nixon went to the South to speak on civil rights at Duke University, a New York Times piece featured an article that Nixon was playing on anti-Catholic sentiments in the South. When the Nixon campaign office was burglarized in early October, a press conference was called to discuss the break-in and the missing files, and the press ignored the incident.

There was the thrill of Nixon's acceptance speech—"I know the

---

[3] The Pilgrims is an Anglo-American institution with chapters both in New York and London. I now serve on its board.

American dream. I have seen it come true in my own life." (Presidential pundit Theodore White called this address one of the best convention speeches in history.)

There was the disbelief that Nixon had 'lost' the first debate. My wife and I heard it on the radio and were convinced that Nixon made mincemeat of Kennedy. Afterward, polls of radio listeners confirmed our reaction. A haggard Nixon on TV (he was just recovering from an infection resulting from a knee injury that took him to the hospital) "lost" to the vigorous and tanned Kennedy (Nixon had refused make-up).

There was the bewilderment on learning that President Eisenhower was going to make only three speeches for his vice president—which the press made much of—because it reinforced Eisenhower's gaffe when he couldn't answer off the top of his head what Nixon's achievements were. Later, we learned that Mrs. Eisenhower had made a private request to the Nixons, unbeknownst to her husband, that her husband limit his campaign appearances to three.

There was the anger against the Boss when he refused to go along with President Eisenhower and Attorney General Rogers, who wanted a Justice Department investigation of the voting fraud in Chicago and St. Louis, which might have overturned the results. Nixon's answer was that it would be giving ammunition to the Soviet propagandists who would use it to deride the so-called democracy of the United States.

Still, the Nixon defeat did not derail my own timetable. I never planned to seek a job as a functionary under the Nixon presidency. I wanted to run as a candidate myself.

To that end, I made my home at my aunt's house in Jersey Shore, twelve miles west of Williamsport. Grey Wing Hall had been the family home for four generations. I wanted time, like grass, to grow over the gaping hole of those Bedford years.

My wife and I had an apartment in Capitol Hill, but our legal home was in Lycoming County. As a would-be candidate, I wanted to build up some defenses against any carpetbagger charge.

I joined the Jersey Shore Presbyterian Church (the fifth Humes generation to do so), and was initiated as a Mason in the local lodge. Politically, my most advantageous membership was the Lycoming County Historical Society. Because no one else wanted the job, I soon became its president. How could a "carpetbagger" tag stick if I was the expert on local history?

Of course, I had given some stump speeches in Lycoming County for Nixon in that year of 1960. During the spring, the Williamsport congressman, Al Bush, died, and a Republican caucus to select the GOP nominee in the special election met in April.

Bush's only legislative achievement was the passage of a Little League Baseball resolution. Williamsport is the birthplace of Little League Baseball. Congressman Al Bush was no scholar, but he knew how to read his Bible Belt rural constituency.

Some pols used to tell the story about how every election year Bush would advertise in one of the rural weeklies in the eight upstate counties he represented. He would place the ad right in the columns that featured the sale of old tractors or young bulls.

LOST—FAMILY BIBLE
Last seen in the front seat of my 1950 Chevy while
driving through the county. Used for daily inspiration.
Please return—no questions asked.

Having evoked the religious and sympathy vote, it never failed to pile up his Republican plurality in that county.

To succeed Bush, the caucus selected a respected Gulf Oil distributor, Herm Schneebeli, whose greatest claim to fame at that time was that he had roomed with Governor Nelson Rockefeller at Dartmouth.

But the Democrats put up a handsome, politically experienced, young Williamsport lawyer, Dean Fisher, as Schneebeli's opponent, and this once-safe GOP district was in jeopardy.

The Republican National Committee dispatched me and Mike Gill, the nephew of President Eisenhower, to recruit Young Republican volunteers for Schneebeli. Privately, my toughest job was keeping the charming Gill out of the beds of the Young Republican women he was recruiting.

A week before the election, Rockefeller flew in to campaign for his old roommate. I managed to be the driver in motorcades through some of the key towns in the district, and so I would report back to the Nixon office the names of the GOP politicians who were offering to help Rockefeller in a presidential campaign against Nixon.

Schneebeli squeaked in by in a narrow margin.

I also took the stump that fall at various rallies for the Nixon–Lodge ticket in Lycoming County. One of my lines to the country folk was that "in the early depression years, the Nixon family sometimes went to bed without eating their supper, but never without reading the Scripture!" I would also mention that Nixon's grandfather, Samuel Brady Nixon, was named after a former Lycoming County Indian scout, who once said after a fight with an Iroquois, "I was scalped but not kilt." In some speeches, I would close:

> Nixon's grandfather died in the Battle of Gettysburg. You can see his grave, which is close to the spot where Abraham Lincoln would say, "Government of the people by the people and for the people shall not perish from the earth."

In the big rally of the campaign when Ambassador Henry Cabot Lodge spoke on the Court House steps, I sat next to Mrs. Lodge and was introduced as "a key Dick Nixon aide" (which of course I wasn't).

The funniest experience I ever had sitting on the dais with GOP dignitaries had happened a few years before. It was Bean Soup Day in Snyder County—a tradition began by the Grand Army of the Republic. A thousand central Pennsylvanians would gather to hear a noted Republican orator. This time the speaker was Bill Livengood, a three-time Pennsylvania secretary of the commonwealth under various governors.

The private life of the Bible-thumping Livengood would make Bill Clinton seem celibate by comparison. Livengood was a rural Jim Curley in charm and oratory. There I was, sitting near George Bloom, the state chairman and "Mr. Republican" of Pennsylvania. Bloom was miffed at the delay in the ceremonies.

Livengood, who hoped to be the party's choice in 1958 for governor, slowly made his way through the crowd, pressing women's hands, saying, "Pray for me, dear" and "May the Lord bless you, sister."

Bloom, watching with distaste, leaned over to LeRoy Greene, deputy postmaster general under Eisenhower, and said, "Here comes Bill Livengood with his Bible in one hand and his cock in the other." Bloom didn't know the loudspeaker was on. The remark, which would be recounted across the state, killed Livengood's future in Pennsylvania politics.

You might wonder how I could keep up with my law school lectures and case studies while spending so much time in Pennsylvania. The answer was Jerry Don Williams, a tall, gangly student with a cowlick in his hair and a slow Oklahoma drawl in his speech.

Today, he is known as J.D. Williams, one of Washington's legendary lobbyists. (He would appear as himself in the Eddie Murphy movie *The Honorable Gentlemen* in 1992.) At law school, Williams would Xerox notes of all his class and case notes for me and then, before the exam, would brief me in all-night sessions.

The only time I ever beat him in a law school grade was in Civil Procedure. It strained the bonds of friendship when my grade mark—just above his—was the highest in the class. The professor, Orville Walburn, was one of three Republicans on the faculty of the law school. And because my wife had worked in the Eisenhower White House in the patronage office before moving to Nixon's office, I was able to have a letter framed from Eisenhower saying that Walburn's name was under consideration for a federal judicial appointment. To the disgusted Jerry, I argued, 'Well, I did know federal procedure—the procedure for appointing federal judges!'"

J.D. Williams, Chuck Manatt, and I were the political trio at law school. Manatt was head of the National Young Democrats. I was an aide for Nixon. Williams was taking notes for both of us, sure to have friends no matter whether Nixon or Kennedy was elected. As a former senatorial aide, Williams knew how Congress worked. And he never forgot the name or, for that matter, birthday of any key staffer. He would scrounge money for flowers for a secretary's birthday or cigars for a staffer's Christmas gift out of his meager pay.

"It's easy to get autographed photographs for yourself of the senator to put on your wall," J.D. would say, "but autographs don't mean access. It's the secretary who gets you in to see the senator."

Little things count. As a young Washington lawyer working with an Atlanta-based firm, he went to the managing partner to ask for a favor. It seems that Carl Albert—then Democratic majority leader—had asked him if he could arrange his daughter's campaign to become Cherry Blossom princess. When William's request was refused, he quit. In the end, Albert's daughter, partially due to J.D.'s handling of the press, won.

At this time, I was working as a speechwriter in the Nixon White House. A big utility conglomerate asked if I could help in a proposed tax legislation that would cost the firm many millions in tax dollars.

I told them that as a member of the White House I couldn't get involved, but I would recommend a lawyer. "We don't need another law firm," said my Philadelphia caller. "They've all struck out!"

'Look," I said, "you have nothing to lose," and I gave him Williams's name.

Later in the week, my Andover- and Yale-educated friend for the utility company called me and said, "This guy's not only a kid but a hick from Oklahoma."

"You know," I replied, "it's nice that congressional chairmen don't hold someone's regional accent against him."

"But..."

"Yes," I said, "it's nice that key congressional leaders who come from Arkansas, Oklahoma, and Texas overlook the fact that a lawyer didn't go to St. Paul's and Princeton."

Silence—my message had finally registered.

Williams, who was then working on a card table out of a friend's closet, went to Albert. He had never told Albert that he had quit his firm to help his daughter, but word had eventually leaked out.

In the conference proceedings to reconcile the House and Senate versions of the tax bill, a provision was added rescuing the company. That's when Jerry became J.D.—he now had his first six-figure yearly retainer.

We didn't belong to the same party, our backgrounds had nothing in common, but we both liked pricking the pretentious and pompous in Washington's political theater.

Williams hadn't left his Atlanta-based firm when I came to the Nixon White House in 1969 as a speechwriter and was subjected to the standard security check.

One FBI agent called on Williams to verify my character. Williams was ready when the brown-suited, white-shirted agent entered the office. Williams had put up photographs of Democratic Party icons like Roosevelt, Kennedy, and Martin Luther King.

Again and again Williams assured the G-man of my integrity and moral rectitude. But occasionally he would shake his head and add, "But there's one thing..." Finally, the FBI agent demanded that he tell everything—it was his "duty as an American."

"Well, he's a fanatic about Nixon," J.D. said, and then elaborated.

The FBI agent dutifully scribbled down this Democrat's assessment of Humes's right-wing proclivities.

Then Williams added, "You know he's a little nutty about the flag—he used to fly it from his house in Williamsport. Why, he's the kind of guy who knows all four verses of the Star-Spangled Banner—he goes a little crazy on this patriotic stuff."

As soon as the agent left the office, he called me for a drink.

"Wait 'til Bob Haldeman reads of your obsessive loyalty to Nixon and your superpatriotic tendencies. Hell, unless the FBI tries to recruit you itself, you ought to be cleared in record time." He was right!

Chapter Seven

LEGISLATIVE CANDIDATE

The harder matched, the greater victory.
HENRY VI (3)

I t was not Nixon's loss in 1960 that would upset my political timetable. It was a win by Al Bush, Jr., son of the late congressman. Young Bush had beaten the Democratic incumbent in the legislative seat I was planning to run for in 1962. My only option was the Williamsport seat for the General Assembly. Unfortunately, the seat was held by a Republican. To challenge him meant changing my residence to Williamsport and then waging an uphill primary fight. So, we rented a Williamsport apartment in time to vote for the municipal elections in November 1961.

There were many, many barbershops and church suppers, but my feet would be my formula for victory. Still, when I first announced, I felt like friends said they had felt during the first days of their divorce—naked and vulnerable.

Here I was, not even graduated from law school, without a job, a resident of the city for only three months, running against "Doc" Whittaker, an established Republican figure who had practiced as a dentist in the city for over thirty years.

For once, I was shy and embarrassed when I called on the eighty-odd committeemen and women for support. After all, I was running against the organization—*their* organization.

One committeeman was an old black man who lived in a shanty near the railroad tracks. Abraham (Bee) Wilson was a onetime boxer and proud member of "Mr. Lincoln's Party." My brother Graham and I called on him to seek the Republican votes in that ward.

"Come in, gentlemen. Would you like a cup of coffee?" We sat in front of his potbelly stove and drank his coffee. (My brother surmised that he was testing us to see if we would drink from a "colored man's" cup.)

I talked earnestly about my legislative goals. Bee was impassive. Finally, I asked him for his support. He looked me squarely in the eyes, stood, and prayed. "Almighty God, I pray that this young man is half the man his daddy was—because if he is, he'll be the best we've seen in years." I later learned that my father had arranged for him to spar in the YMCA which had been closed to blacks. (Bee and about a third of the Republican city committeemen and committeewomen would buck the Republican organization to support me.)

On the roof of the van which my brother bought for me for $200 was perched a leather-backed chair with a sign saying "Fill the Empty chair in the Assembly—Elect Humes." The empty chair was to remind voters of my opponent's absentee record in the State House. (Our Mercedes was safely parked twelve miles away.)

I couldn't attack Doc Whittaker, who had a conservative record, but I could nail him for votes he hadn't made. I took out full-page ads in the daily newspaper with the headline: "DOC WHITTAKER FAILED TO VOTE 42 TIMES FOR VETERANS."

Then the next day: "DOC WHITTAKER FAILED TO VOTE 32 TIMES FOR TEACHERS."

At first, the Williamsport *Sun-Gazette,* which was vehemently against me, refused to take the ads. Finally, their avarice overcame their antipathy, particularly when I backed up the ads by detailing in fine print the date and page numbers of the Pennsylvania House

Legislative Journal. The ads were signed by a group calling themselves *Citizens for a Full-Time Assemblyman.* Those ads, plus the empty chair, so riled Doc Whittaker that he put a baby carriage on top of his Thunderbird, saying, "DON'T SEND A BOY TO DO A MAN'S JOB." I countered by organizing a march of mothers with baby carriages bearing signs that said, "Mothers for Humes."

Then along with the attack ads, I wrote positive copy promoting the pluses of Humes. I should put it in the singular—because there was only one. I would be "full-time."

In the talks before the twenty or so coffee klatches we had, I developed the speech device of "negative name-dropping."

I would drop the name of former President Eisenhower or Vice President Nixon in an anecdote that made fun of me. It was a way of referring to my work in the White House or Nixon's office without bragging.

"I was very close to one of Vice President Nixon's best friends. I used to scratch Checker's ears..."

"There I sat outside the presidential office, dressed in a three-piece suit, with my leather briefcase, as if I were a cabinet official instead of some part-time gofer, when President Eisenhower emerged. I stood up so quickly that I knocked over my briefcase, and my apple and bottle of Coke rolled out in front of the president's shoes..."

In these *Meet James Humes* coffee sessions set up in various neighborhoods, I would sometimes jibe at my opponent's experience. "I'm well aware of my opponent's senility—I mean, seniority," I'd say with a smile.

Despite the advertising war waged in the newspaper, confrontations between me and my opponent were few. One was to the Republican women of Loyalsock Township. At the community hall where the debate was to be staged, the women brought their casseroles to the buffet table.

To my dismay, I found that I was to go first. My prepared remarks were framed to answer Whittaker's attack, and I did not relish attacking him first. It would not only reinforce the sympathy for Whittaker, whom they had come to know over the years, but it would also justify his personal attacks in response to me.

I rose, uncertain of what I should say. So, I began by praising the baked bean casserole of one Republican hostess. When I saw her beam, I lauded "the pineapple marshmallow surprise" of another. Suddenly, realizing I would alienate the women whose recipes I didn't extol, I continued, piling praise after praise on the culinary concoctions—chicken à la king of one, the meatloaf of another, the raisin–apple pie, the carrot cake....

I closed: "You are the source of any success in Harrisburg I aspire to. I will follow your recipe—one measure of old-fashioned honesty and one measure of hard work."

Doc Whittaker rose to the bait. "I'm a serious legislator. I came to talk about issues and not someone's cooking recipes." The audience cooled. They were proud of their prize dishes, and at least "that nice young Mr. Humes appreciated them."

Another venue was the churches. Just before the collection in the Pine Street Methodist church Doc Whittaker attended, an announcement was read each Sunday on Christian activities and events—at the end of which was an announcement from Mrs. James C. Humes, executive secretary of the Williamsport Council of Churches. That drove the good doctor up the wall. "Now that kid," he'd rant, "is putting ads in my own church!" (Judge Greevy, a popular figure like my father, had secured the job for my wife.)

Just before Primary Election Day in May, I had another debate with Whittaker. He opened with a blistering attack, saying that "Humes was a carpetbagger" who doesn't even own any property.

When it came my turn, I said, "You know, I don't think it matters whether you first came into this district with your clothes on or clothes off," and went on to give my three-point plan for expanding job opportunities.

Then I closed, "No, I don't think it matters whether you are a native Williamsporter or own property. But, as a matter of fact, I am a native, born in this city almost twenty-eight years ago, and my opponent is not. He moved here after dental school.

"And, as a matter of fact, I do own property." I opened my coat and unpinned a sheet which I unfolded twice to reveal a two-foot-wide document.

"Here is the deed to Wildwood Cemetery where my family rests and [my voice breaking] so, God willing, will I some day." My brother, who was sitting in the back, said he almost threw up—but I left with resounding cheers.

On the Sunday just before the election, I got a call from Charlie Mahaffie, the county prothonotary. Mahaffie was a popular courthouse figure who never endorsed or campaigned for anyone other than himself. The one exception was me. "Your daddy brought me into politics," he told me, "and I'm going to support his boy."

Every Friday night, I stood by him at Williamsport's central shopping corner beside a Liggett's Drug Store and on Saturday morning at the Farmer's Market. (Those were his spots, year in and year out.) He'd introduce me to those who walked by—he knew thousands by name. "You might remember Judge Humes. I want you to vote for Judge Humes's son."

Mahaffie had a printer friend who had leaked to him that a scorching editorial was coming out Monday afternoon accusing me of being a lawbreaker. It seems that Loyalsock Township had an ordinance against posters on electric wire posts, which I had been unaware of.

I called Tom Gerber, the manager of what people were now referring to as the "Humes machine," and twenty of us went out in the wee hours of Monday morning to tear the posters down.

The *Sun-Gazette* had to revise its copy.

Election Day found me depressed, even if both my brothers—who came in for the long weekend—as well as my wife were upbeat. The upset victory was all the more sweet for it.

I spent most of the summer in Philadelphia boning up at a cram school for the bar exam. That July afternoon when I finished my eight-hour ordeal, I was giddy with relief. I noted that the Trocadero, an old Philadelphia burlesque house, was featuring "Miss '48'," which didn't allude to her age! And that her manager was Lord Moynihan. Could it be Tony Moynihan, my old Stowe friend who had married a Persian belly dancer? I had to find out! The first time I had ever seen a burlesque show was at the Windmill in London—with Tony's father, Lord Moynihan.

To my right was Lord Moynihan's (his father had died some years before and he had inherited his seat in the House of Lords) newly betrothed, a sexy nymphet, his former secretary, my friend's step-mother-to-be, not quite two years older than I. And to my left (appropriately!) was Lord Moynihan's friend Harry Pollit, head of the British Communist Party, an old Marxist gadfly who tried to pro-voke me with attacks that Ike was a "capitalist tool" of Big Business.

Tony Moynihan, however, loved America. That's why he had sought me out at Stowe. So I proposed to my eccentric English chum that I give a reception honoring him and his bride. Who would turn down an invitation to a tea for Lord and Lady Moynihan?

Some doyennes of Philadelphia's Main Line accepted. I intro-duced my guests of honor to the invitees.

"And this is Lady Moynihan, Mrs. Cadwallader." Tony's new wife wore a V-cut sequined gown parading her voluptuous assets.

The Main Line matron was aghast. When one dowager asked what she did, Lady Moynihan answered in an accent worthy of a pre-Higgins Eliza Doolittle, "I'm in the arts, dearie." Because of my fête, I was forever blackballed by some of Philadelphia's bluebloods.

(A postscript to my erstwhile zany schoolmate. He died in the Philippines in 1993, the husband of a Manila madam of a bordello—his fifth wife. Today, two of his sons have sued to inherit his seat in the House of Lords, one the son of the madam and the other a child by a Filipino dancer whose record of marriage is questioned.)

When I returned in September to the political hustlings, I had problems with Williamsport's elite establishment. My Democratic opponent was a handsome Episcopalian gentleman and former prosecutor who was endorsed by the county sportsmen and NRA.

He was going to cut my margins in the posh Republican wards, so I had to take Democratic votes from him in the Italian river wards and the Polish wards.

Most of the Republican organization was now behind me. Their advice? Tie yourself to the popular GOP candidate, Bill Scranton.

But the straight ticket rationale, I thought, was weak. I had to make them want to vote against Bob Wise. The problem was that he was a nice guy.

So, I met the argument straight on. For a full-page advertisement, I coined this banner headline in screaming type on top of the page: "BOB WISE IS A NICE GUY BUT..."

Then, I had a picture of the double doors of the Democratic caucus room in Harrisburg. One door I had labeled "Philadelphia" and the other "Pittsburgh"—the big cities.

Another version of "the Big City" control message showed Wise in handcuffs, each manacle with the imprint of Philadelphia and Pittsburgh.

Once again, as in the primary, I hit the neighborhoods in my truck.

In the 11th ward, a Polish-populated and heavily Democratic district, a middle-aged slightly balding man answered.

I began my usual spiel. "Mr. Wyrostek. I'm James Humes and I'm running for the assembly."

He interrupted. "Don't you know who I am?"

"Aren't you Mr. Joseph Wyrostek?"

"Yes, but I'm a Democrat."

"I know that but I'm calling on all homes, Republican as well as Democrat, because I want to represent all views."

"You still don't understand—I'm the Democratic ward leader."

"Yes, but I'm still calling…"

"Let me tell you something, young man," he interrupted. "You're going to be the first Republican in a long while to carry this ward, but you won't be carrying it, it'll be your dad.

"I worked against your dad when he ran for judge, and a couple years later my wife and I ran into hard times. One day in November, a coal truck pulled up at my house and I told the driver, 'I didn't order that.' The driver said, 'It's already paid for.'

"I didn't find out 'til later that it was your dad," and his voice broke as he added, "and I never got a chance to thank him."

His word was good—I did carry the ward.

Daddy, who could speak a bit of Italian, was the first non-Italian to speak on the Italian-speaking radio hour every Sunday. So, I was invited to be interviewed in Italian. Because of my study of Latin and some visits to Italy, I could make a stab at Italian.

Near the end of the hour, I was asked what part of Italy I liked the best. I was on the spot—I didn't want to offend anyone's homeland.

I replied, "Mi piace Roma, mi piace Firenze, mi piace Napoli, mi piace Calabria, mi piace Sicilia…"

The next day I took a call at my home.

"Signore Humes—why you no like Abruzzi?"

If I won, it would be without the Abruzzi vote.

On November 4, contrary to my expectations, I scored a relatively easy victory, no doubt helped by the landslide victory of Bill Scranton.

Chapter Eight

LEGISLATOR

Get the glass eyes:
And like a scurvy politician seem to see the things thou dost not.
KING LEAR

hen I was sworn in on January 1, 1963, as Pennsylvania's youngest General Assembly member, I did not realize that every freshman member (at least on the Republican side) had to undergo a hazing, or initiation, rite. The initiator was Enos Horst—a rotund, elfin "country boy" whose ruddy cheeks resembled the apples he grew.

"Young chappie," invited Horst, "come back with me to the Porcelain Chamber."

There in the counter beside the washbasin he pulled out a silver flask and poured its clear contents into a water tumbler. "Drink all that down, my young chappie, or I'll block any private road bill or pet project you introduce."

I threw down his distilled applejack that "white lightninged" my innards.

I was a legislator for only minutes and had already broken my first campaign vow not to drink. No one had really pressured me to take that vow. But during the campaign, I had been invited to a tea party. The five maiden ladies who welcomed me into a

Victorian parlor were the officers of the Lycoming County Prohibitionist Party.

"Mr. Humes," the president said, as her calico cat nestled in my lap, "your father always ran on our party ticket as well as the Republican ticket. We'd be honored if you would also run under the Prohibition Party label.

"We won't ask whether you ever imbibe—we know your father was a teetotaler."

"Well, I can't say that I haven't on occasion, but I'm not going to as a legislator."

The funny thing is, when I revealed that pledge to old Enos, he said, "That's okay, Humes. I have their backing, too. You see, publicly, I vote 'dry' but privately, I drink 'wet.'" Indeed, on at least one occasion we had to carry Enos out of the Men's room to vote against selling liquor on the Sabbath.

I had hoped to get a seat on the Education and Cities Committee—everything but Philadelphia and Pittsburgh. I did get those assignments, but I got them before I went to Harrisburg or even talked to fellow house legislators. I got it through "Senator" Harry Princeton Davis, who was Harrisburg's lobbyist for Sun Oil. He was called "Senator" because he had a Senate locker and even a Senate seat and was more powerful than any of the senators.

Joseph N. Pew, long the chief financial angel for the GOP, nationally as well as in Pennsylvania, was the president of Sun Oil Co. (Sunoco) and a Neanderthal Republican. On one occasion, when Pew's name was sounded in the roll call of the convention, he was sound asleep. Convention Chairman Joe Martin again called, "Joseph Pew." Still, the Sun Oil mogul slept on. Martin again barked, "For the third and last time, Delegate Joseph Pew!" Groggily, Pew responded, "I vote for General... General... My vote is for General Grant."

Joe once had great hopes for my father and had touted him for both governor and the State Supreme Court. I told Mr. Pew and Senator Davis what committee I would like.

As I came out of the office with Joe Pew, an old codger, who looked a lot like one of today's homeless in a disheveled, brown overcoat and a moth-eaten wool cap, said, "Hello, Mr. Pew." To my astonishment, Mr. Pew responded, "Reds, how are you? How's Molly?"

"Fine," Reds answered.

"Do you need any money?"

"No, thank you, Mr. Pew," he said as he tipped his hat and shuffled off.

Pew turned to me and said, "That's the only honest politician I ever met." He then related that in December 1936, his secretary informed him that Mr. Maloney wanted to see him. Pew answered that he didn't know a Mr. Maloney. The secretary added, "He says it's a personal matter of some urgency."

Maloney was shown in.

"Mr. Pew," he said, "you don't know me but I'm a ward leader in Fishtown [a district in Philadelphia]. Like all of us captains I received $300 for 'walking around money' [the term for precinct get-out-the-vote funds] for Governor Landon. Now, Mr. Landon is a Christian gentleman, but I knew he didn't have a Chinaman's chance against President Roosevelt, so my wife and I took our first trip—we never could afford a honeymoon—and we went to Florida, and here's the $27.00 that's left."

I had come to Harrisburg with starry eyes, but the smoke-filled rooms soon clouded that vision.

One of my political beliefs was that a representative, as British statesman Edmund Burke said in his famous Bristol address, "should not sacrifice his judgment to his constituency." This is the "trustee" theory. Since the public always wants more benefits and lower taxes, the legislator is, in a sense, a judge who has to weigh which measures to support. I did make an exception to that principle: the legislator should be a delegate, not a trustee, on mores issues. In other words, the public opinion of the district should rule on such issues as tobacco, alcohol, and Sunday sales. One such mores issue was gun control. A League of Women's Voters lady called on me in Harrisburg:

"James, I know you, like your father, to be an educated man. I want to tell you some facts about the dangers of having guns."

I quickly said, "Don't confuse me with the facts. I don't own a gun, but I'm not going to vote for gun control. Why, if there was a referendum in Lycoming County offering an either/or for castration or taking away their rifles, the men in this county would probably choose the former."

But I followed the trustee theory on Governor Scranton's bill to raise the sales tax. The Republican House was not eager to pass the measure. At dinner with legislators, I argued that we'd be better off voting on it quickly—if we dawdled, it would be "like taking a bandage off slowly." The House Majority Leader, Al Johnson, said, "Jamie, why don't you say that on the floor?"

So my maiden address was on taxes. I quoted Shakespeare's Lady Macbeth: "If t'were done, 'tis best done quickly."

A year later, I got my reward. A state trooper brought me my appointment to the Pennsylvania Shakespeare Quadricentennial Commission, serving along with novelists Pearl Buck and Conrad Richter, as well as artist Andrew Wyeth.

I sent my reply back with the trooper:

> Will your grace command me any service to the world's end? I will go on the slightest errand now to the Antipodes that you can devise to send me on; I will fetch you a toothpicker now from the farthest inch of Asia; bring you the length of Prester John's foot, fetch you a hair off the great Cham's beard, do you any embassage to the Pygmies.

A week later, a terse reply came back from the governor: "Jamie, you are making 'much ado about nothing'!" That indeed had been the title of the Shakespeare source.

Another approach by a state policeman that year was not so happy. An extended meeting in Philadelphia threatened to make me late for my Assembly duties. I was tearing westward on the Schuylkill Expressway when I heard the siren.

The young, handsome trooper stepped to my rolled-down door window. I read his name tag and immediately promoted him. "Officer Simchek, I want to commend you to Commissioner Purdy," head of the Pennsylvania State Police in Harrisburg at that time.

"What?" said the confused trooper.

"Too many officers don't stop legislators when they see the HR license plate. After all," I pontificated, "those of us who make the laws should obey the laws."

"Well, Representative," Simchek stammered, "I do think you were speeding..."

"If you say so, Officer, I'm sure I was. Frankly, my mind was not on the speedometer."

"It wasn't?"

"No, I'm the sponsor of HR 1188, and the importance of that vote which takes place this afternoon was all that I was thinking of."

"That's the state police pension bill?"

"Yes, but I think your duty demands..."

Simchek went back to his car. I could hear him talking by radio to his supervisor.

"I have Representative Humes here—he's the sponsor of HR 1188—he was speeding—he says he's trying to get to Harrisburg for the bill..."

"Simchek, if you don't want to be permanently stationed in Coudersport [the upstate Siberia], you get in Humes' car, leave yours at the road, drive him to Harrisburg, and don't go under eighty."

With the trooper drivers of other state police cars saluting my chauffeur, we made it two hours before voting.

Like that pension bill, most of the legislation is pretty mundane. As I said before, most of the time being a legislator means being a judge: you're deciding between two "litigants"—oculists versus optometrists, funeral directors versus cemetery owners, registered nurses versus practical nurses. With little to go on except your gut instincts, you have to decide. The oculists charge that blindness could be caused by a misreading by the optometrist—the optometrist counters that he can do for $9 what the oculist charges $100 to do.

The party seldom takes a position on these kinds of bills in the caucus. Issues like taxes, school reorganization, and teachers' salaries are different.

The most controversial bill in my tenure was reform of Unemployment Compensation, an all-out war between business and unions. Labor was fighting to keep the status quo. The Republicans said union members were "double-dipping" and that Pennsylvania could attract business only by eliminating the excesses.

It was the only time my house was picketed. The local union leaders, who dominated the Democrat Party, even offered a free pass for my reelection—that is, no opponent in 1964—if I bucked my party to vote against the bill.

One uncommitted Republican legislator was from Johnstown, where Bethlehem Steel had been constantly laying off workers. Death threats forced him and his wife to be moved by the Pennsylvania State Police to a secret site. On the date of the vote, he had to enter the hall under police guard. His vote was the margin of victory. He never ran again.

There is a myth that money changes hands on these kinds of votes. If it did, I never heard anything.

One night, I was having a hamburger in the Harrisburg Hotel and heard a legislator from a rural western county complain to Adam Bower, a longtime legislator.

"Adam, I've been here six months, and no one has ever offered me any money."

Bower feigned surprise. "You don't tell me, Ross. Where do you stay?"

"In the Penn Harris."

"Always the same room?"

"Oh, yes, 324 always."

"You keep your transom open?"

"Why no, Adam. Why?"

"Hell, that's how they drop in the envelope."

A month later all of us legislators were in Harrisburg for the Pennsylvania Banker's Dinner. Bower said to Ross:

"Don't look now, Ross, but there'll be a big fat Ben Franklin under your plate."

My colleague couldn't wait. During the invocation he peeked under his plate and then said, "Jesus Christ, Adam, they forgot me again!"

Bower, who never got a high school degree, was chairman of the House Appropriations Committee. He represented Northumberland County, whose czar was Henry Lark, the Republican Party chairman. In the late 1930s, when Lark's Republican assemblyman died, Lark paid the jail fine and costs of Bower (Bower had been charged with drunkenness and battery) and ran him as his candidate.

In Harrisburg, only two things mattered to Bower: Lark's instructions and his pension.

One day, I looked at the calendar, and the bill for the day was the Civil Service Reform Act. I was puzzled because that bill had never even been discussed in the daily caucus meeting. Just then, Bower leaned back to say, "Humes, good government bill—pass the word to freshmen legislators—good government bill—you can't be against it."

I was suspicious. Bower and "good government" were incompatible. I read the bill and found in the small print a legislative pension raise. My smelling a rat was confirmed when I saw Bower flick the electric toggle switch to register "yeas" in empty seats, including that of my friend Karl Purnell, who was back home getting out his weekly newspaper, which he owned and edited.

In his editorials, Purnell had earlier come out against a pension increase. Using his fictive skills (he later became a playwright), he worked out a rationale for his switch in a new editorial.

Karl's entrance into the Harrisburg scene, incidentally, had been triumphant. On Inauguration Day, he rode forty-five miles from his house to the Capitol on his white horse.

Karl Purnell introduced me to Governor Nelson Rockefeller's Godkin Lectures at Harvard on "The Future of Federalism"—a call to reinvigorate state governments as an antidote to big government in Washington.

I pontificated on this philosophy at a Lincoln Day dinner in the nearby rural county of Montour. Afterward, the crotchety county chairman took me aside. "When you come here again, Humes, just remember there are only three things to speak on: for Guns, for God, and against Philadelphia."

If I had no expertise in guns, I was conversant with God and the Bible. With my bit of Greek at Williams, I could read, albeit with a dictionary, the epistles of the New Testament as Paul wrote them, as a guest preacher at rural churches.

As superintendent of the Sunday School of the First Presbyterian Church, I heard the fears of members when the Supreme Court in 1963 banned prayer in the public schools. My wife, as executive secretary of the Council of Churches, was inundated with letters.

In March 1964, I had the governor of Oregon, Mark Hatfield,

as a guest in my house. In my letter of invitation for him to speak at our Chamber of Commerce, I offered him, in addition to his fee, a chunk of the original piece of the U.S. Capitol Building—which I had received from Vice President Nixon (when the front facade was extended, the remnants of the original structure became available).

While Hatfield was my guest, a group calling itself the Christian Businessmen Council rang three times asking to see the governor. I knew it vaguely as a conservative fringe group and dismissed the callers, until Hatfield, who overheard me the third time, said he would like to meet them. At breakfast at my house, the handsome Hatfield looked like a model for Brooks Brothers—striped, rep tie; button-down shirt; wing tips.

After we had talked about the prayer-in-school issue and a constitutional amendment, one of the Christian businessmen asked, "Mark, when did Jesus first call you?" To my astonishment, my urbane guest answered, "I was dean at the University of Williamette, and Jesus said 'Mark, I have a mission for you.'" Those words came from a national political figure whom I had heard nominate Nixon in the 1960 convention and who was slated to be the keynoter for the coming 1964 convention in San Francisco.

Hatfield's religious fervor did not dim his realism of political facts, however. He said, "Jamie, opposing Goldwater is a waste of time. He already has the votes."

The nomination of Goldwater, whom I respected for his principled conservatism, also, I knew, dimmed my chances for reelection.

My bid for the religious vote was a resolution memorializing Congress to pass an amendment to allow parts of the Old Testament to be read as literature in the public schools. After all, the Bible, like Shakespeare, is part of our literary heritage. A newspaper release invited Sunday schools to send petitions to me.

Just as hundreds of names on petitions were pouring into my office, I received an invitation to attend the Presidential Prayer Breakfast at the Mayflower Hotel with President Johnson and Doctor Billy Graham.

If I attended, I might get a great "photo-op" of my presenting the petitions to Johnson and Graham. Before the breakfast, I told the photographer to be quick since the Secret Service might block me from handing anything to the president, and I went in to the breakfast. I found myself seated next to Ted Kennedy. Poor Ted—I kept him busy all breakfast autographing prayer programs to Democratic committeemen and women I knew! I never told him I was a Republican.

During a lull in the proceedings, I grabbed the petitions (I had them under my chair) and made for the head table. "Mr. President and Doctor, here are petitions for Bible reading." No sooner said than the Secret Service restrained me. The photographer was able to get off one shot, not a good one, showing LBJ with the startled look of someone about to be shot and a puzzled Billy Graham.

The coverage in Williamsport had one negative protest. A constituent called to register his opposition on constitutional grounds.

"Do you represent a group?" I asked.

"Yes, Lycoming County Atheist Society," he replied and began to inveigh against "breaching the wall of church and state."

After five minutes, I praised him. "You certainly stated your case very well. Have you thought of writing a letter to the newspaper?"

Some days later, a letter from the Lycoming Atheist Society appeared in print. Atheists, like Arabs, are welcome adversaries for politicians.

Richard Nixon once told me the fatal sin for a politician is to be boring. Despite his advice, my speeches at first were just that— a litany of issues like some shopping list. I soon learned to talk about only one topic—be it education, economic development, or transportation needs—and cover the other issues in Q & A.

The hot topic in the spring of 1964 was the presidential campaign of our popular governor.

When Governor Rockefeller withdrew after his defeat in the California primary, our Governor Scranton, after a meeting with General Eisenhower at Gettysburg, announced.

But the general was not supporting Scranton. His aides had inflated his encouragement to seem like an endorsement. When pressed by reporters, Eisenhower reasserted his neutrality.

A group of us legislators called on the general to urge him to change his mind. The press, which had depicted the aging Eisenhower as a befuddled old man, had no idea of his political astuteness.

"Gentlemen," said the general, "it is no secret that Goldwater is hardly my choice. My brother Milton is heading Bill Scranton's presidential campaign, and my son John is mobilizing volunteers for him, but I promised neutrality in early 1962, and I'm going to keep that commitment. Of course, at that time I could not conceive that Dick Nixon would lose the governorship in California or that Rockefeller would get divorced.

"Well, Goldwater now has the votes locked up, and I'm not going to throw away whatever influence I might have on him as the Republican nominee by actively fighting against him in a hopeless cause."

Eisenhower then pulled out a map. Every state had pins, mostly blue, a few red, denoting delegates.

"Gentlemen, the red ones are those I think I could change with a phone call. If there were enough of them, I would break that pledge of mine and call them. But there are not enough."

The fight to derail the Goldwater bandwagon may have been quixotic, but I signed up to volunteer for the Scranton presidential campaign.

William Scranton was one of the most popular governors in the history of Pennsylvania and deservedly so. In a profession that seems to attract both bloated egos and quivering insecurity, Bill Scranton was a patrician with style and character.

In June, as one of Scranton's "ambassadors," I boarded a plane in Philadelphia bound for San Francisco. It was loaded with VIP Republicans. Through the babble of political voices, I heard the bell-like tone of a female English accent. It has always drawn me like the sirens did Ulysses.

The voice in the back row of the plane belonged to Lady Jean Campbell, granddaughter of British press mogul Lord Beaverbrook. Beaverbrook, a wartime cabinet minister under Churchill, had two dailies to propound his Tory views—the *Daily Express* and the afternoon tabloid, the *Evening Standard*.

Lady Jean, whose age, as well as her bra size, was in the late thirties, had Senator Javits as her rapt audience. She was telling the senator she was covering the Republican Convention for the *Standard*. I introduced myself and quickly established some various British friends at Stowe and some who had been aides to Churchill.

To Senator Javits's dismay, the high-spirited Lady Jean shifted her attention from him to me.

When our plane landed for a stop in Los Angeles, before replaning to San Francisco, we were delayed for an hour by a bomb scare. As we waited in the plane, I came up with an idea for her first report. I even wrote the lead for her: "My knickers [English for "panties"] were riffled today to see if there was a bomb."

She confided that she had no hotel reservation. I found her one in mine—a third-rate hotel, a far cry from the posh St. Francis or Mark Hopkins hotels. We then cabbed over to catch Henry Cabot Lodge at a press conference at Scranton headquarters. I knew that Lodge would not miss recognizing Lady Jean as I scrambled to find a place for her in the front row.

Lodge, who had been a write-in victor in the New Hampshire primary, stumbled over the endorsement he read for Governor Scranton. He did worse at the Q & A that followed. Despite his tenure as senator and U.S. ambassador to the United Nations, he was a disappointment when Jean and I got some private time with him. An imposing figure, he is proof that a great name, a fine pedigree, handsome looks, and an English tailor is all it takes for success in politics.

Now that she had material for her second report, we taxied off to Ernie's famous eatery on the waterfront. She had finished her second martini when Stewart Alsop, who had met her in London, spotted her. He came to our table and invited us to a party at his suite that night at the St. Francis. Later, as the waiter brought us our cioppino and salmon, she grabbed my hand and said, "Jesus, Jamie, we have to clear out. He'll kill you."

"He" was Norman Mailer, her estranged husband, who was covering the convention for *Esquire*. Until that moment I didn't know she was married—much less that she was married to Norman Mailer. I needed no convincing. I had read a year back that a drunken Mailer had stabbed a man in a jealous fit.

Quickly, we raced to the kitchen, upsetting one waiter and tray. Out the kitchen door we fled.

That night we went to Alsop's suite. It turned out that we were the only guests. Alsop soon made it evident that "two's a party, three's a crowd." I never saw her again.

I always assumed that it was with Alsop that she found her lodging for the rest of the week. Lady Jean never would win awards for her journalism, but her libido, looks, and love life with the famous might have earned her an entry into Guinness's Book of World Records. She reportedly slept with three heads of state in a year, an alliterative trio—Kennedy, Khrushchev, and Castro (JFK at her place in Georgetown in October 1963, Khrushchev at his Russian dacha in April, and Castro in Havana in May).

After a few hours on the floor at the Cow Palace, it took only a few minutes to realize that the heart and soul of this convention belonged to Goldwater.

After buying all the postcards in the St. Francis and Mark Hopkins hotels, I repaired to the Scranton policy suite and sat it out writing postcards with my friend, Jim Reichley, a former Scranton staffer who was covering the convention for *Fortune*. Reichley, for years a Fellow at Brookings, was resident historian of the Republican Party and its philosophical direction.

One person who was impressed by my taking the time to write was the Princetonian who headed the Collegians for Scranton, Tom Kean. Years later I would help him draft both his gubernatorial inaugural in Trenton in 1982 and his keynote to the GOP convention in 1988.

I did pause to hear Goldwater's acceptance speech when he split the Republican convention wide open with these words: "Extremism in the pursuit of liberty is not a vice, moderation in the pursuit of justice is not a virtue." I told Tom that it sounded better in Greek when I read just about the same words in Plato.

Afterward I paid a call on Rockefeller's campaign office and got to see Jack Welles, the New York lawyer spearheading the Rockefeller forces.

"Mr. Welles," I urged, "it's a mistake for Rockefeller not to endorse Goldwater. He can make it a *pro forma* endorsement of the Republican Party and then spend the fall campaigning for moderates like my old boss Senator Ken Keating, who is facing Bobby Kennedy. If he doesn't endorse him, he won't have a chance of being nominated in 1968."

He didn't, and I was proved right.

If Rockefeller ever considered supporting Goldwater, the selection of Congressman Bill Miller from his own New York State quashed that chance.

Congressman Miller—who later won dubious attention posing

as a "forgotten man who needed his American Express card"—
would come to Williamsport in late October. Though I supported
the ticket, I ducked being on the platform. To the good GOP
ladies who later asked why, I said I had been invited to speak at
memorial services for Herbert Hoover who had died a few days
earlier. Of course, I had myself arranged the service.

My opponent, chosen after Goldwater had been selected, was
my former opponent Bob Wise. At our two debates, we talked as
if we were campaigning for two different offices. He praised the
record of JFK and LBJ, and I lauded the record of Governor Bill
Scranton.

Defeat on election day did not come as a surprise. Though I
ran ahead of Senator Hugh Scott in my district, the LBJ landslide
was too much. At the age of thirty, I became a statesman—an
involuntarily retired politician.

Chapter Nine

BARRISTER

Keep on the windy side of law.
TWELFTH NIGHT

I n less than two years, I had graduated from law school, bought a home, become a father, and won and lost an office. I now had to pay the mortgage and sustain my family.

It was a slow but interesting process. One day a political client walked off the street and into my law office. He wanted me to represent him in a wage dispute with a former employer. When I asked him for a retainer, he stormed out saying, "You're a cheap bastard! Your father didn't even charge me!" I pointed out to him that if Sam Humes was my father, I couldn't be a bastard!

Curiously, it was my father, along with a fellow Harvard Law graduate, Marshall Anspach, who founded the Lycoming Legal Aid Society in 1929.

About a month after the society was founded, an old codger was thrown into jail. The homeless coot had crawled into a farmer's chicken coop for some shelter on a winter night. For his supper, he had killed one of the coop's tenants, which he then grilled over a fire.

Such an egregious crime demanded swift and stern justice, and the district attorney was up to the challenge. He charged the chicken murderer with trespass, breaking and entering, and larceny.

At one point in the trial, the prosecutor asked the defendant, "Did you ever serve in prison?" My father objected, and the judge called a "side bar" conference at the bench away from the jury's ears.

The decision agreed on in the conference was to let the question be answered but that the judge would instruct the jury, before they adjourned for deliberation, to disregard any prison sentence in its considerations.

The prosecutor then repeated his question.

"Did you ever serve in prison?"

The grizzled defendant managed a faint "Yes."

"Where?" the prosecutor followed up.

"Andersonville, Georgia," the old fellow squeaked. "I was a member of the Bucktail Regiment."

A gasp was heard from the jury. Andersonville was the Buchenwald of the Civil War, and the Bucktail Regiment was the Pennsylvania Honor Guard unit that had been singled out by Lincoln for its valor.

My father didn't even bother to refute the commonwealth's evidence. But when it came for his summation to the jury, he turned to the flag hanging in the courtroom and began counting all the stars. "... forty-five, forty-six, forty-seven, forty-eight," he concluded.

"Forty-eight of them—not thirty-four—because of the sacrifice of that shell of a man you see on the stand. Don't you think those two years in Andersonville where he was beaten and starved are punishment enough?"

Despite evidence to the contrary, the jury came in quickly with a verdict of "Not Guilty."

The Samuel Johnson notion that "patriotism is the last refuge of the scoundrel" had little resonance in Lycoming County.

One old lawyer made a specialty of defending World War II veterans on any criminal charge. When word was circulated that Ed

Toner was representing a veteran, lawyers would fill the courtroom to hear this pint-sized, dapper attorney give his summation to the jury. It always began with those Continental Army soldiers at Valley Forge, "their shoeless feet, nekked and bloody…" Down through history he would continue his roll call of courage, through the Civil War's Gettysburg and World War I's Ardennes Forest, and ending with the raising of the flag at Iwo Jima. It almost never failed to elicit tears and an acquittal from the jury.

That and his speech on the trial of Christ were the only weapons in Toner's forensic repertoire. His portrayal of the Sanhedrin's prosecution of Jesus in Jerusalem was his rhetorical tour de force at church suppers, where he always managed to pick up a client or two.

One case where I was a public defender involved both God and the flag. Isaac Martin was a nineteen-year-old Mennonite who had refused to register for the draft. This plain-clothed youth was not protesting against the Vietnam War. (The war in early 1965 was only beginning to stir opposition.)

Isaac could have registered as a conscientious objector, but chose not to register at all. If he was afraid of what the government might do to him if he failed to register, he was more frightened of his father if he did. His father, Abraham, was the bishop of his small church. Abraham Martin looked like an old Civil War photograph of John Brown—coal black eyes from a gaunt face stared angrily not only at the prosecutor but at me and my partner in the case, Beth Kury.

Abraham Martin did not trust any "Englander," especially Englander lawyers who were "agents of the devil." The government was a "war machine," and any connection to it was an affront to his conscience.

With his father driving the horse-and-buggy, Isaac Martin, along with his mother and two sisters, came north to Williamsport for the trial and tied the horse to a parking meter in front of the building that housed the federal courtroom.

In a sense, what took place were three epic conflicts. First, there was the lonely individual against the might of the state.

The second pitted the eighteenth century against the twentieth, symbolized by the buggy parked next to the cars of the judge and prosecutor.

The third conflict was the relationship between father and son, which was symbolized in their biblical names. The biblical Abraham, in the book of Genesis, was ready to sacrifice his own son, Isaac, in obedience to God. Abraham Martin, to prove his own faith, was ready to yield up his own son to prison. Isaac Martin was more afraid of violating his father's precepts than the laws of the state.

Both the federal judge and the jury were sympathetic to the soft-spoken, ruddy-cheeked Mennonite who looked years younger than his twenty years. The docket that week had been filled with cases of chiselers on relief checks, forgers of Social Security checks, and the like.

Before the trial began, the judge implored the youth to register as a conscientious objector. If he did, the case would be dropped, and an almost certain federal prison sentence would be averted. Isaac looked at his father and then shook his head.

With a weak case, we constructed a defense based on duress. At that point, the U.S. attorney threatened to indict both father and son for conspiracy to break a federal statute, which carried a heavier sentence. We had to change our rationale for duress.

I put Martin on the witness stand.

"Why did you not register for the draft?"

"It breaks God's commandment."

"What is that commandment?"

"Thou shalt not kill."

"You know that as a conscientious objector you won't have to kill anyone?"

"Ya."

"So why not register?"

"Because I would be part of the engine of your government, a killing machine."

"What happens if you break God's commandment?"

"I go to Hell."

Over the prosecutor's objections I asked,

"What is Hell? Say in your own words what Hell is."

"A lake of fire."

"How long are you put in this lake of fire?"

"Forever. Eternity."

To the jury, I laid out in the words of Milton and Dante the fiery hereafter that Isaac Martin really believed he would be condemned to if he violated God's commandment.

Before the jury retired, the judge instructed them to disregard my statement and consider only whether the statute had been violated.

Eventually, the jury came back to the courtroom, and the foreman said in a faint voice, "We find the defendant guilty." He was given a one-year sentence.

It was not the last time I would represent a client who had a fear of the supernatural. In 1965, I was called into Judge Greevy's office. He handed me a letter from a resident of a mental institution in Danville. George Spotts, whom I never met, had specifically requested me as his counsel.

Spotts was not a poor man. In fact, his money was the cause of the dispute. Since his institutionalization, his relatives had taken his estate away from him. Spotts wrote in his letter that he knew "a lot more about the market and investments than those thieving relatives of mine."

The problem with Spotts was his paranoia. He believed that Jewish and Catholic demons had taken over his body.

He had chosen me, he had said in his letter, because "as Sam Humes's son, you have the purest blood of any lawyer in the county," a blood "not contaminated by any Jews or Catholics."

Off I drove to Danville to visit my client. Spotts, who bore an avuncular mien, enthusiastically greeted me. He reminisced about my father and asked about my mother. I asked him about his financial holdings. He rattled off the latest stock market quotations of his many securities. And then, as I began to inquire about his savings accounts, he interrupted. "Mr. Humes, I know you have pure blood, so you won't laugh when I tell you that Jewish and Catholic witches are operating these electrical gadgets on my body. Why, when I take a piss, it's Jewish or Roman piss.

"You got to stop them, Mr. Humes. If you don't, they'll soon be polluting all pure Americans."

"Mr. Spotts," I countered, "let's first win the case that you are financially competent. If we win that, we'll be in a stronger position to consider the other matter."

"If you think so, Mr. Humes."

The courtroom drew a lot of lawyers. Word had circulated that my client might even attack the judge for allowing this Jewish and Catholic witchcraft to operate in Lycoming County.

Before I put my client on the stand, I read to the court several commonwealth decisions stating that insanity did not prove 'financial incompetence' and that such competence should be determined by the subject's capability to manage his affairs.

I then put Mr. Spotts on the stand. He was a walking *Standard and Poor's*. I had him recite the number of shares he had in various corporations and the closing quotations of their worth.

Then I put into the record the *Wall Street Journal* of the previous day, which confirmed his testimony. Spotts smiled at the astonished looks of the courtroom audience.

But after I finished, the judge asked, "George, is there anything else you'd like to add?"

"Yes, Your Honor. These Jews and Catholics have been operating these machines…" And on he went.

After the court delivered its finding against George, I sat down with him outside the courtroom.

"George," I said, "I told you not to get into that other matter."

"I know, Mr. Humes, but when the judge asked me, I just had to answer. I have one favor to ask."

"What's that, George?"

"That you charge a whopping big fee—every penny you get is one penny less for my cheating in-laws."

Another time, I had defended a Lycoming College senior who, on a steamy June day, wanted to get off campus and out of the city to celebrate his release from the college regimen. He drove alongside the Loyalsock Creek, turned off onto a dirt road, crossed a stream, and decided to cool off by taking a dip. Quickly, he stripped.

The creek hardly came to his waist, but he let the rushing stream wash off the day's sweat and dirt. After a while, he heard a giggle. He glanced to his left and sighted two pairs of eyes. A closer look revealed two young girls peeking behind some trees. He acknowledged their presence by a wave as if to say "Hi, girls, I see you."

The girls fled. Days later he was slapped with charges of "indecent exposure" and "corruption of minors." Apparently, the two sisters, late for their chores, told their parents that a naked man had made advances to them.

The twenty-one-year-old graduate saw his future shattered. As an education major, he had hoped to teach school. A conviction would end that career before it started. He also was an ROTC student, and a guilty verdict might force him to give up his officer's commission.

Any cross-examination of the two girls required the sure but delicate skills of a brain surgeon. I had to undercut their charges without triggering a collapse into tears.

The prosecutor and I agreed that the two girls would give their testimony separately. As far as cross-examination went, I usually rejected the harsh inquisitorial approach of some lawyers. This time, I wanted to be particularly careful. Since my size lends itself to an overbearing presence, I try to compensate by being a gentle bear.

I interrogated the older girl first, tried to put her at ease. I exacted from her that she was late that June afternoon in helping her mother to peel potatoes. Then in the softest and most sympathetic tone I could muster, I asked her again to describe where she was in the woods, what she saw, how much she saw, and what was the exact gesture the accused made.

Later, I put the same questions to the younger sister.

Their answers varied greatly. The older sister testified he said, "Hi, girls," and waved with a circular motion of his hand. The younger girl deposed that he said, "Come on in, girls," with a forefinger beckoning. The older girl admitted she was in the woods for five minutes watching. Her sister said the two had hardly spent a second in the woods before the accused startled them.

The case was dismissed.

One day, Judge Abe Lipez from Lock Haven told me of my father's style in the courtroom.

"There I was," the judge said, "three years out of law school, dressed in my suit from Jacob Reed [the upscale clothing store in Philadelphia], and arguing for my client who was suing some manufacturer.

"Your dad said to the jury, 'Mr. Lipez is a brilliant lawyer. He crafts his legal points well, just like that fine suit he wears.'

"Of course, he was really saying that I was a slick, smooth-talking fancy-dressed lawyer.

"Look, Jamie, I was the poor Jewish boy who came up the hard way—your dad was the one born with a silver spoon in his mouth. But your dad knew how to come off almost as a bumbling country lawyer, as if he hadn't gone to the Hill School, Williams College, and Harvard Law."

If I played the teddy bear in the courtroom, I was a grizzly in my office—at least when representing the accused as a public defender. I learned from sad experience that the criminal class lies, even to its own lawyers.

"Mr. Humes," said one accused who had been sent in by the

Public Defender's office, "I swear I wasn't even there at the Triangle Tavern. I was home that night watching television. May God be my witness."

Then, in the trial, the DA produced three witnesses to his knifing at the Triangle Tavern.

So, I forced myself to say things to my client like, "You can't expect me to believe that..." or "Stop lying to me," just to make sure how I could best represent him.

The criminally accused that I dealt with fell into three categories—most of them thought they were smart and weren't, some really were clever, and a few were so dumb that they were marginally moronic.

It is this last type that the Supreme Court, Gideon ruling in 1960 really helped—the kind so stupid and terrified that they can be manipulated by the police to confess even if they are innocent.

I remember saving one slow-witted man with a cleft palate who had been charged with stealing a bicycle. He had been scared into confessing when he was innocent. On the opposite end is the career criminal who knows just what chords to strike in his hymn of repentance. I represented one of these in a parole hearing. "Mr. Humes, I can't sleep at night when I think of the young man I killed. I've prayed to Almighty God that if I get out, I'm going to devote myself to Jesus and to helping the juvies [juveniles] to understand that breaking the law will break the soul...." I won his parole, and he was back in prison three months later.

Such criminals are more than immoral—they're amoral. This particular criminal had heard that I was in Yokefellows, a group formed by the late Elton Trueblood,[4] for prison ministry. And the prisoner thought, if that's this attorney's thing, I'll ring that bell.

A lot of the criminal class are sociopaths who have either lost their conscience or never had one. Most of those I saw in the criminal

---

[4] Chuck Colson now heads this group.

trials couldn't hide their deficiency, but some were smart enough to conceal it and say what they thought you believed in.

Take a situation where you see a $20 bill fall out of a guy's wallet. You'd return it to the owner, but the not-so-smart sociopath doesn't believe anyone would return it if no one was looking. The clever criminal, however, knows that those deciding his fate are among those who would return it.

At a parole hearing, a prisoner I had represented wailed a dirge of repentance and renewal. After he was turned down, I said, "Williamson, I thought you laid it on a bit thick."

"Mr. Humes, if people believe in Santa Claus and the Easter bunny, I'm going to talk Santa Claus and Easter bunny."

I once submitted a book proposal for publication with a working title of *The Tales of Two Cities*. The paired cities were Seattle and Vancouver, Minneapolis and Winnipeg, Buffalo and Toronto. The rate of crime in the Canadian cities versus the American cities ranged from a quarter to a third less, even though Canada shares with us the same jurisprudence and the same common law. The differences are more.

But when you suggest some of the reforms that Britain, Canada, and Australia have adopted, my lawyer friends blurt out that "that could lead to Nazi Germany." Well, I haven't yet noted storm troopers marching in London, Toronto, and Sydney.

Churchill was once invited to participate in an event celebrating the American Revolution.

"What revolution?" he scoffed. "It was Englishmen fighting for their rights as Englishmen—English-speaking people fighting against a Hun king and his Hessian hirelings—not the last time that English-speaking people would fight against German despotism."

If it was a revolution, why do we still cite as law British cases that happened after 1776? The man who tried to assassinate Ronald Reagan was convicted under the McNaughton rule—an English common-law case of an attempted assassination of Prime Minister Robert Peel in 1814—some decades after our Declaration of Independence.

An elderly woman from Philadelphia's "Main Line" once came to me. She was long in lineage but short in funds. She couldn't pay her hospital bill. But she told me that a friend of hers had told her, "Don't worry, Cissie, I'm going to leave a bequest to a Bryn Mawr hospital to take care of my friends like you." I checked up on it. Sure enough there was a legacy "to provide for ladies of gentle birth in indigent circumstances." The hospital solicitor argued that anyone could allege that he or she was of "gentle birth" and that it was inoperative because of "vagueness."

I found a common-law case in 1832 that defined gentle birth, and she qualified. Today, I also can claim gentle birth because I can now meet the test, which is: produce the maiden names of your four great-grandmothers. She could, and I can now. (The mothers of my four grandparents are Flora Sebring, Caroline Lamphier, Elizabeth Fleming, and Jennifer Penhale.)

The best job I ever had was as executive director of the Philadelphia Bar Association. I had left Williamsport in 1966 to become legislative counsel for the Greater Philadelphia Chamber of Commerce, having been recruited by Thacher Longstreth—a Philadelphia civic institution, who would one day write his own autobiography, *Main Line Wasp*.

Longstreth had come to Williamsport to speak in January 1962, but I was elsewhere taking law exams when Longstreth spoke to the Lycoming County Young Republicans, ending with a plea for young people with ideals to enter government. Then he added, "I'm thinking about young men like your own James Humes." At that moment, Representative Doc Whittaker, who was at the head table, jumped up and said, "If I had given that long-legged son-of-a-bitch a hundred dollars, I bet he would have mentioned my name."

Three years later, in 1965, I had to decide whether to regain the seat I had taken from Doc Whittaker in 1962.

My decision was not to run.

Small-town life was too restrictive—the uphill ascent from

representative to state senator to Congress demanded the discipline of a marathon runner.

In 1966, the Philadelphia Bar Association job opened up. I left my job in the Philadelphia Chamber.

In my bar association office in the annex of city hall, I sat underneath portraits by Benjamin West of such notables as George Mifflin Dallas (the vice president under Polk, for whom Dallas, Texas, was named). I was my own boss. I wrote a column each week for the Philadelphia legal journal, the *Daily Intelligencer*, and a commentary each month for the association magazine.

I used my legislative experience to lobby in Harrisburg for a new state constitutional convention and sat on boards recommending judges. I also presided over the Legal Defense Operation (civil representation for the needy).

This was the oldest continuing bar association in the world, predating even the Constitutional Convention for which it had provided research. Suddenly, I had more offers for speeches and demands for articles than I could fulfill. Perhaps it was a job without a future, but it was fun.

Chapter Ten

NIXON CAMPAIGNER

It might be the pate of a politician—one that will circumvent God.
HAMLET

I wasn't planning to go to the annual Pennsylvania Society Dinner at the Waldorf in New York in 1967. It was a dinner in those days mainly for Pennsylvania Republican politicians. I was an ex-politician, or at least an ex-legislator. This dinner, Pennsylvania's biggest political dinner, had its start in the late nineteenth century when the New York City banks hosted their major clients from Pennsylvania—the steel, coal, and railroad corporations. In turn, those same corporations footed the bill for those friends who especially favored them—the Pennsylvania Republican legislators.

In December 1959, I rode for the first time the "Pennsylvania Society Express." That was the name given to the Pennsylvania Railroad's special train from Pittsburgh via Harrisburg to Philadelphia and on to New York. I got on with my brother Graham in Philadelphia, and when we got off in New York, we had to help carry a drunken Supreme Court Justice to a cab. The free booze—courtesy of the Pennsylvania Railroad—was responsible for many unsteady gaits across Penn Station.

If the event today is bipartisan, in the early sixties it was virtually a

Republican party affair. Just before a gubernatorial election year was the best time to attend. The big counties hosted receptions for their favorite sons. The December following the election was also a must for aspirants looking for appointments by the incoming governor.

In one of our visits in 1961, my brother and I had looked down from our dining table in the balcony to see Elkins Weatherill, a scion of the Main Line, standing awkwardly all by himself in the front dais, stiffly holding the fifteen-foot pole of a Pennsylvania flag. After some titters from the dining multitude, the embarrassed Weatherill withdrew.

What had happened was that Thacher Longstreth, the close-to-seven-feet sprite, had grabbed the flag off a stanchion, when he had spotted Weatherill out of the corner of his eye. Weatherill asked him, "Thach, why are you holding that flag?"

"Didn't George Bloom [the GOP state chairman] call you, Elkie?"

"No."

"Why, that's strange—anyone who is a political Republican candidate for governor or senator is always asked to hold the Pennsylvania flag."

Weatherill, then a township commissioner in Montgomery County, was positioning himself for a gubernatorial run, and he said:

"Damn it, Thacher. I've raised pots of money for the party on the finance committee, and yet they ignore me."

"I agree, Elkie, it's not fair," replied Longstreth, who was hoping to get the party nod for senator. "You hold it—you've far more reason to carry it than I."

"No, I wouldn't think of it, Thacher."

"I insist. I couldn't look myself in the mirror if I carried it and you didn't."

So that was how Elkie ended up on the stage all alone holding the flag, with his patrician countenance as red as a fire engine.

Still, in the block-long Waldorf lobby stretching from Lexington to Park Avenue, one could measure the power of Pennsylvania pols by the size of the coterie around him. There was one oleaginous lawyer I always considered my own personal power barometer. I would boom out, "Hello, George!" when I saw him next to Hugh Scott or some other Republican VIP. In 1959, when I was considered close to Vice President Nixon, he was warm. The next year after Nixon's defeat, he brushed me off. In 1962, after my election to the State House, he was effusive. In 1964, after my defeat, he barely mumbled my name.

As I said, in 1967, I was not planning to attend the festivities, until a call from Dick Nixon changed my mind. I was asked to wrangle an invitation for his law partner, Tom Evans. The purpose was to establish contact with potential delegates to the Republican Convention in Miami the next year.

The irony was that the featured speaker at the Pennsylvania Society dinner that year was Governor Nelson Rockefeller, who at that point looked like Nixon's chief rival for the presidential nomination. Senator Hugh Scott and Governor Ray Shafer had wanted to showcase Rockefeller to Pennsylvania Republicans. Unfortunately, as a speaker, Rockefeller had the windiness of a Bill Clinton and the woodenness of a cigar Indian. While he was reciting his accomplishments like names in a telephone directory, I had no problem coaxing diners away from their tables to chat with Dick Nixon's law partner.

Among the commitments we garnered for Nixon was GOP patriarch George Bloom and Congressman Jim Fulton from Pittsburgh. Fulton, one of the most liberal Republicans in the House of Representatives, had entered Congress with Nixon in 1947. He had an affection for Nixon. As a ranking member of the Foreign Affairs Committee, he had always admired Nixon's international expertise. At the Miami Convention, Fulton would bring a western bloc of delegates with him against the opposition of Governor Shafer.

I was now back in presidential politics, even though as head of the

Bar Association, I was supposed to be out of it. During the previous year, I had worked with Arlin Adams, the chancellor of the Philadelphia Bar Association. In January 1968, his term was over. I persuaded Arlin to head the Nixon campaign. Adams had served as Pennsylvania's secretary of welfare under Scranton. A Philadelphian of Jewish faith and a moderate Republican, Adams was a respected leader with strong links to the Scranton, Shafer, and Scott wing of the party.

I had told Arlin, "You belong on the Supreme Court. Rockefeller won't be nominated, and Dick Nixon will." He blanched at mention of the Supreme Court.

"Well, that's not the reason, Jamie. I'll be for Dick Nixon because he's the most qualified candidate." Adams would be appointed to the Court of Appeals and upon retirement in 1990 would serve as a special prosecutor. Twice, he was the front runner for a Supreme Court appointment, first by Nixon in 1970 and then by Ford in 1976. Both times he was nudged out through barrister backstabbing by those who should have been his friends. (It is a regret of mine that one of the finest men I have known in terms of character and intellect did not serve on the Supreme Court.)

Don Whitehead was sent to help me in my behind-the-scenes management of the Nixon campaign in Pennsylvania. He would be the coordinator of the Mid-Atlantic states. Don was from the Boston area, but the Nixon organization deliberately chose operatives out of a local area to run campaigns in order to avoid the thorny thicket of ideological and factional jealousies.

Don, an honors graduate in English from Williams, looked and dressed like a Teamster truck driver. He preferred the company of Beantown, Massachusetts, politicos to stockbroker country clubbers like his father.

In 1968, the Northeast was the home of liberal Republicanism. Whitehead's job was to sign up support for Nixon. That meant prying away potential delegates from the clutches of the state organizations in control of moderate Republican governors and senators.

Pennsylvania, for example, was dominated by Governor Ray Shafer and Senator Hugh Scott.

Don and I called on Shafer in Harrisburg to tell him that if he chose to be a "favorite son" candidate and not commit to Rockefeller, we wouldn't challenge him in Pennsylvania. Shafer assured us that he had no intention of committing. Afterward, Don shook his head. "'No intention' is a political weasel word."

When Shafer did endorse Rockefeller, he applied his club of patronage power—thirty thousand state jobs and state contracts—to enforce it. Still, Whitehead, with my help, got the pledges of about thirty people willing to buck the state machine.

In New Jersey, despite the Rockefeller endorsement by State Chairman Webster Todd (father of current Governor Christine Whitman) and U.S. Senator Clifford Case, he signed up Hap Farley, the Republican boss of Southern New Jersey who led twenty-two delegates into the Nixon camp.

The media in 1965—not for the first time—misread the national political situation. They saw Rockefeller as the main threat to Nixon. As Nixon told me at the time, "If I'm beaten, the candidate will be the governor of a big state—but it won't be Rockefeller, it'll be Reagan." That's why Nixon early on signed up Strom Thurmond and Barry Goldwater. In the South and in conservative enclaves in the West, the hatred of the New Yorker Rockefeller was far deeper than the affection for Nixon.

Nixon told his campaign chairman John Mitchell that if he didn't win on the first ballot in Miami, "the slippage to Reagan could begin with a trickle and end in a flood."

By the time we arrived in Miami for the convention, Don and I were telling uncommitted delegates that Nixon had the first ballot nomination locked up. We'd say, "The train is leaving the station, and you'd better get on it now."

I remember working on the socially ambitious wife of one conservative ideologue from western Pennsylvania. As the liaison between delegates and the Eisenhower family, I would arrange meetings with John, Barbara, and David Eisenhower.

My pitch to her was made at the inaugural parties where, I assured her, she would make lifelong contacts. To his wife's and my surprise, her husband voted for Reagan. When the Shafer people saw that he was about to go for Nixon, they cornered him and said, "Follow your conviction, and vote for Reagan."

The projected majority for Nixon on the first ballot was razor thin. To be nominated, Nixon had to keep in line the votes of the Nixon delegates in Rockefeller-dominated Pennsylvania and New Jersey.

The Rockefeller forces came up with an anti-Nixon ploy clothed in the guise of Republican unity. Their pitch: "Let's prevent the infighting between Nixon and Rockefeller which will wreck any chances for Republican unity in the fall." Rockefeller Republicans in Pennsylvania and New Jersey would then propose favorite son candidates—Governor Shafer in Pennsylvania and Senator Clifford Case in New Jersey.

In response, Whitehead met with Atlantic City boss Jim Farley. The chain-smoking Farley said, "I'll call them [the New Jersey delegates] right now." He did, and the Case balloon was punctured. In Miami, Scott, Scranton, and Shafer triple-teamed Arlin Adams and begged him to support Shafer in a unity slate. Adams acquiesced.

I had a call from George Bloom alerting me to the Adams agreement. I called Don, and he called John Mitchell. Mitchell subjected Adams to a series of Anglo-Saxon expletives the gentlemanly Adams had probably never before heard. Adams's assurances to Scott and Shafer were rescinded.

Newsweek later reported that the defections in New Jersey and Pennsylvania were the difference that delivered the nomination to Nixon on the first ballot.

I watched the Wyoming delegate put the nomination over the top from the Nixon hotel suite. On the coffee table before me were notebooks on each of the potential vice presidential candidates. The media had almost convinced me that Nixon would pick the moderate Senator Mark Hatfield to balance the ticket.

But the Nixon briefings that I read revealed that the ideal ticket from the Nixon vantage point was Nixon–Nixon—no tilting to the left or right. The proof was that Nixon's first choice was Lt. Governor Robert Finch of California. I had worked under Bob Finch when he was the chief of staff for Vice President Nixon in 1960.

The only commitment that Nixon made regarding the second spot was that Strom Thurmond, representing the South, would have a veto. Nixon once told me, "Jamie, the guy who elects presidents is the guy who owns his own home but not a college degree."

In a two-man race, Nixon knew he could beat Vice President Humphrey. The Democratic Party was deeply divided by Vietnam. Nixon's pitch to the country was, "A man who cannot unite his party cannot unite the country."

But George Wallace threatened to take away the good old boys from the South and the blue collar workers from the North. None of the vice presidential recommendations I read included Nixon's personal choices—Governor John Volpe of Massachusetts and Governor Spiro Agnew from Maryland, the former of Italian background, the latter Greek. Both were ethnics who would attract traditional Democratic urban votes in the North but would not scare away the South.

Agnew got the nod. Agnew had earlier endorsed Rockefeller, but had angrily withdrawn his support when Rockefeller, without calling Agnew ahead of time, had dropped out of the campaign in March—only to reenter after the primaries closed. In May, when Agnew had put down ghetto riots in Baltimore, he earned national press recognition. That coverage would make Thurmond and the South opt for the border governor Agnew.

Twenty years later, I was still drawing from my experience at the Miami Convention. At a black-tie dinner on the Main Line of

Philadelphia to raise money for a local International House, I found myself seated next to the hostess, the second wife of a newly minted software millionaire. The blonde-coiffed spouse tried to ennoble her husband's millions by enlisting herself in every cause from saving the snail darter to helping the homeless. She turned to me and said, "James, you've spent a lot of time in Washington. I'm deeply involved in the nuclear freeze movement—what do you think?"

Actually, I held the nuclear freeze movement in minimal esteem. A limited detente had been worked out by Nixon with the Soviets in the SALT talks. Self-interest had convinced superpower Russia to sign an agreement. But nuclear freeze was essentially unilateral disarmament by the U.S., while there still loomed Khadafy of Libya or the ayatollah of Iran, who were outside of any disarmament treaty enforcement.

I assumed what my daughters call my "five-star pontifical baritone." "You know," I intoned, "that subject came up when Winston Churchill and Dwight David Eisenhower were my guests for dinner, and the thinking was this..." and I proceeded to give my own opinions.

My twelve dinnermates sat in rapt silence.

Some weeks later, I encountered in downtown Philadelphia one of the dinner guests, who was a prominent lawyer as well as a Democratic Party activist.

"Humes," he said, "you are so full of crap. What's all that about you having dinner with Churchill and Eisenhower?"

"Why didn't you say anything?"

"Well, I know you've done a lot of things, and about 90 percent of the things you say you've done you've actually done, but my wife and I while driving back in the car started figuring out your age and that of Churchill and Eisenhower...."

"Let me tell you how it happened," I interjected. "Back in the Republican Convention of 1968, I was a liaison with the Eisenhower family and potential delegates. One morning I spotted Winston

Churchill II, the grandson who was covering the convention as a journalist. I had met him and actually visited him and his wife in his home in Hayward Heath in Suffolk a few years previously. So, I invited him to dinner that night with David Eisenhower [Dwight David Eisenhower II].

"In the middle of our threesome dinner at the Diplomat Hotel in Hollywood, apropos of nothing, I began listing a whole litany of problems—the future of NATO, the world population explosion, nuclear disarmament, the Common Market, world trade…

"And then young Winston Churchill interrupted, 'Humes, what on earth are you talking about? You're not making any sense.'

"'Oh,' I said, 'I just want to be able to say that the subject came up when I was having dinner with Winston Churchill and Dwight David Eisenhower who were my guests for dinner and the thinking was…'" My friend, the Democratic lawyer, said with disgust, "That's worthy of your hero, Nixon."

The press has always fed the speculation that General Eisenhower did not like Nixon. They point to the press conference in 1960 when President Eisenhower could not reel off the top of his head a list of accomplishments by his vice president, or that Eisenhower did not socialize with the Nixons when he was vice president.

In truth, Eisenhower did prefer those of his own generation for companionship and, like most career soldiers, he harbored a distrust of career politicians—he had spent many Washington years as a military bureaucrat playing up to influential congressmen and senators.

Still, when Nixon lost in 1960, Eisenhower said it was the blackest day of his life, with the exception of the death of his first child in 1925. Eisenhower had trained Nixon to be president by making the vice presidency into a meaningful office. Nixon acted as his deputy chief of state abroad by visiting foreign capital in Europe, Asia, Africa, and Latin America, and at home he played the role of deputy head of party by assuming most of the political campaigning.

He thought that in 1960 and 1968, in terms of his knowledge and experience in foreign affairs, Nixon was the most qualified person in the country. The only minus on the Nixon ledger was his electability. Shortly before he died, Eisenhower predicted wrongly that Nixon would not be reelected. "Dick," he said, "knows how to win the people's respect but not their affection."

In 1968, I worked with David's father, Colonel John Eisenhower, running the Citizens for Nixon campaign in Pennsylvania. John was the president, and I secured Theodore Roosevelt III as chairman.

I would have run the regular campaign in Pennsylvania but for one person, Ray Shafer, the governor. Until the Nixon campaign, I always had warm relations with Shafer. He had stayed at my house on a couple of occasions when he was lieutenant governor. I had struck up a friendship with his daughter, Diane, who shared my love of Scotland. (She had attended the University of Edinburgh, and I had married in Edinburgh.)

In early 1967, we had hosted a party, complete with bagpipe, for Diane and her Scottish fiancé Ian Strachan in our Philadelphia home. In May, Governor Shafer came to Philadelphia to address the Bar Association (I wrote his speech). In the lobby of the Bellevue-Stratford, Diane asked if my wife and I had received an invitation to a dinner party at the summer governor retreat at Indiantown Gap. We hadn't.

A month later at the convention in Miami, I ran into Diane again. She said, "Jamie, you haven't answered my invitation for the Indiantown dinner."

When I returned home, I asked my wife if she remembered seeing such an invitation. She hadn't. I called the governor's social secretary to accept, even though I could not locate the invitation.

A little later she called back to announce coldly, "Mr. Humes, you are not invited." I put in a call to Diane, and she said, "Jamie, you come or I'll never forgive you—and you're going to be the guest of honor."

When I arrived, Diane took me to her father. "Daddy, I don't care whether Jamie is for Dick Nixon, George Wallace, or Adolph

Hitler—don't try to play politics with my friends." And an abashed Shafer spluttered, "There must have been some mistake."

But, anyway, I was vetoed to run the Pennsylvania campaign for Nixon. A Hugh Scott lieutenant, Dave Maxwell, was picked. Nixon did not carry Pennsylvania. George Bloom, Mr. Republican, maintained to his death that if he and I had run it, Nixon would have won the state.

George Bloom, in my presence, later complained to Nixon in the Oval Office. "Mr. President, only two Nixon loyalists ever got jobs in this administration—Jamie Humes and John Eisenhower. The rest were Scott people."

In August, John Eisenhower called me to come quickly to Washington. General Eisenhower had suffered a stroke.

I parked my bag at the apartment of Mike Gill (Mrs. Eisenhower's nephew), but I spent most of the night with John Eisenhower at his suite at Walter Reed Hospital. It was touch-and-go that night. After a late dinner, we started making plans for a contingency funeral. With tablets as cars laid out on the floors, we set up a motorcade with various VIPs and started to sketch out the service.

John Eisenhower, by the way, is a first-class military historian who has the discerning eye for detail of a novelist. Those who doubt that the general was very bright should have spent time with either John or Milton, the president's brother, as I did. Intelligence was not lacking in the Eisenhower genes.

Fortunately, General Eisenhower survived that stroke, although he would never return to Gettysburg.

A Nixon–Humphrey debate was scheduled in September on the Rosemont College campus, pitting Colonel John Eisenhower against former Governor Endicott ("Chubby") Peabody of Massachusetts.

At the last minute, John, who hates the limelight, backed off and sent me in his place. When I worried about my substitute appearance, Don Whitehead repeated to me the Massachusetts old joke: "Governor Peabody has two cities named for him—Peabody and Marblehead."

But, in credentials, I was overmatched by the former Massachusetts governor, so I crammed on the material fed to me by Nixon
headquarters in New York as well as on Peabody's background.

Peabody laced his spiel with the pitch that Nixon, in President
Johnson's words, was "a chronic campaigner..." "a two-time loser...
" twice repudiated by the voters."

I waited until the end of my address to offer this closing: Turning
to Peabody, I said, "Chubb, a great man once wrote, 'Only in the
ordeal of loss is the mettle tested—only in the crucible of defeat is
character defined.' That man was the rector of Groton, your grandfather, Endicott Peabody. And Dick Nixon, tempered by trial, forged
in conflict, has the requisite leadership to guide our nation."

The grave of Franklin Roosevelt's Groton headmaster must have
suffered seismic shocks as I invoked his name to support Richard
Nixon.

Yet, the most bizarre endorsement I engineered was from another
man of the cloth. This one would endorse Nixon after his death!

Through Gail Pendleton, a longtime friend and contributor to
Nixon, I was asked to speak to Father Divine's flock. Father Divine,
so I'm told, was in person a small, unimposing black man of light
complexion who, in the pulpit, was transformed into a charismatic,
thundering presence.

Franklin Roosevelt detested the black preacher. Divine had
instructed his followers to vote for Wendell Wilkie in 1940. Not
only did he back Wilkie, but he also erected a neon sign on the
home he bought opposite Roosevelt's Hyde Park estate that flashed
"No Third Term."

Nixon headquarters in New York had sent me Nixon's speech
entitled "Black Capitalism." I arrived with two Nixon aides to
deliver my address. It didn't take me more than a few minutes to
decide to scrap the suggested remarks. The Father Divine disciples—
about three-fourths black and three-fourths women—were far
closer in philosophy to the DAR than to the NAACP.

Many Main Line matrons would hire Father Divine believers only as maids. ("Well, my Magnolia turned over to me a fifty-dollar bill she found in the street in front of our house.") When converted by Father Divine, they would choose new names such as Lotus Blossom and Peach Petal. Scrupulously self-reliant and honest, they refused to accept even federal welfare or unemployment compensation.

At the dinner, I sat at a feast table that was about thirty yards long and piled high with platters of food. (I had been warned by a friend, "Take only what you will eat—to leave food on your plate is an act of disrespect.")

The head of the table was flanked by two jewel-encrusted thrones, one empty, the smaller one occupied by Mother Divine, the handsome white widow of Father Divine. We were greeted by a bass voice emanating from the empty throne.

"God give you greetings. I can see you, but you cannot see me. I have assumed spiritual form…"

As the throng of hundreds sat transfixed, the two Nixon staffers fidgeted nervously in their seats. Then the resonant voice boomed from the throne: "The Apostolic Choir will now favor us with a few anthems." Twenty well-upholstered women in sequined gowns lifted their soprano and alto voices in selections with titles like "Jesus, Let Me Hold Your Hand" or "My Country Tis of Thee." Following the hymns, I was introduced by Mother Divine.

I stood and nodded to the empty throne:

"Father Divine, it is an honor to be in thy
tabernacle…"

From the corner of my eye, I could see the Nixon aides blanche as I continued:

I beseech each of you to stretch out your hands—
further, further—close your eyes. Can you sense it? Can

you feel it? Can you breathe it—it's fellowship, it's brotherhood, it's sisterhood, it's love!

"Amen, Amen, Amen," was the ensuing response.

Then, lowering my voice to a stage whisper:

When I heard those clarion tones from the Apostolic Choir, I thought of Gideon's trumpet outside the walls of Jericho, and I wished that the windows of this tabernacle were not only physically but figuratively open, for then the walls of Atheism, the walls of Agnosticism, the walls of Materialism, the walls of Socialism, the walls of Marxism would come tumbling down.

With resounding "hallelujahs," I launched into my speech, not daring to look at my Nixon monitors:

When the Pilgrims landed at Plymouth Rock, they wrote a contract that began "In the name of God, Amen."

And Thomas Jefferson, sitting at the boarding house at 4th and Market Streets, wrote, "that they are endowed by the Creator with certain inalienable rights…"

And Benjamin Franklin at the Constitutional Convention said, "If no sparrow can fall from the heavens without His notice, surely no nation can rise from the ground without His help."

And Abraham Lincoln, just before he went to Ford's Theater, issued an executive order putting "In God We Trust" on the nickel.

You know, when I served in Harrisburg in the General Assembly, I often had the occasion to look at the mural above the speaker's rostrum. It showed a man reading a document from a balcony. The man was the sheriff of Philadelphia, and the story behind that picture was this—John Hancock, president of the Continental Congress, gave the word to circulate the Declaration secretly, stealthily, surreptitiously, but the Philadelphia sheriff said, "On the bell in the Tower and the words from the Bible, 'Proclaim Freedom to all the world and all the inhabitants thereof.'"

And Sheriff John Nixon said, "I'm not afraid to proclaim the message of freedom," and so John Nixon had the message of freedom proclaimed.

And I ask you to let his collateral descendant Richard carry the message of freedom to the world once again.

Silence followed, and then a trickle of applause that ripened into an ovation. Mother Divine put up her hand and said, "Let us pray."

We all bowed our heads.

"O Father," she implored, "we have heard from this eloquent deputy of Richard Nixon. Tell us, Father, how should we fulfill God's wishes?"

Not a murmur was heard. I opened an eye slightly to look at the Nixon operatives on either side of me who had their hands clasped as if in prayer, but their faces were stricken in grimaces of pain.

Mother Divine broke the silence. "Father has spoken. We should not only give Richard Nixon our vote but also give him our dollars."

A collection plate was passed, and I was handed a round purple sock tied with a gold tassel. Then I was shown to a sedan chair in a litter. I sat down and was carried in Father Divine's litter to his white Cadillac, in which I was driven home.

The next day the black newspaper the *Philadelphia Tribune* blared its headline, FATHER DIVINE ENDORSES NIXON.

In the ensuing years, whenever I saw those Nixon aides, they wouldn't look at me, and gave me a wide berth.

Chapter Eleven

NIXON WRITER

All my best is dressing old words new.
SONNET

’ve been to a coronation and I’ve been to an inauguration, and I can tell you that one has class but the other is kitsch. But you have to go to one to find that out! The year 1969 was that time for me. On that cold January Monday in 1969, we watched the parade from H.L. Hunt’s suite in the Willard Hotel overlooking Pennsylvania Avenue. (The hotel would close after the inauguration, not to reopen until the 1982 Reagan inauguration.)

I had known the billionaire’s son, Lamar Hunt, at the Hill School. Lamar, a soft-spoken, modest gentleman, was the antithesis of his free-wheeling, swaggering father. The billionaire doled out so few dollars for Lamar’s weekly allowance that twice Lamar asked me for a quarter to put in the Sunday church collection. H.L. Hunt did not so much like Nixon as hate LBJ. “Sleazy crook” was one of his milder epithets for his fellow Texan.

That night we went to the white-tie Inaugural Ball. People don’t go to the ball to dance cheek-to-cheek with their spouses; they go to rub elbows with the rich and mighty. Any hopping on the floor they do is table-hopping. I was no exception. One man I spotted at a side table was a familiar face. I couldn't think of his name, but I knew that we had met. I approached him. "My name is James Humes. I can't think of your name, but..."

"Yes," was his dry reply. "When I last saw you, you had your pants off." (We had met at the rental place where we were both being fitted for our white ties.)

I had reason to search the ballroom floor for the powerful. I was job seeking.

Just before Christmas, I had invited J.D. Williams and Don Whitehead to my house for a weekend search of the "Plum Book"—the government publication of all the jobs not covered by the civil service. J.D., who had been a field operative for the losing Humphrey campaign, was the "Washington insider" who would help us look for the choicest plums.

The book did help Don to pick a ripe one for his old boss, the head of a Boston insurance company. It was a spot on the American Battlefield and Monuments Commission. The retiring CEO was required to see that cemeteries were mowed in countries such as France and Italy, in between attending receptions by the resident ambassador. A limousine and chauffeur were supplied for his staff. (For some reason the commission members never see the need to inspect the cemeteries in Tarawa or Attu, Alaska.)

The distinguished businessman was not amused by Don's tongue-in-cheek suggestion that he might look into the Federal Pornography Commission, which paid $200 a day and presumably all you could read or watch!

I was being considered as a general counsel for the Department of Commerce when I got a call from Jim Keogh at the White House for a speechwriter's job.

Keogh, a former magazine editor of *Time*, professionalized the speechwriting operation at the White House. Under LBJ, it had been a freelancing operation. Johnson, himself, would hand out the assignments—sometimes giving the same speech job to two or three people—convinced that two heads were more apt than one to come up with memorable lines. The result, though, is a splice job—that is, a speech that's the equivalent of a quilt.

I had done little in the way of actual writing for the Nixon campaign operation out of New York. I was hired originally for my notebooks of historical anecdotes and quotations. To that file I added more to the cross-quotesmanship lines of liberals whose statements would echo and buttress Republican points.

I also came up with a new gambit, which I called "global gamesmanship." Since it would sound self-serving for Nixon to vaunt his own foreign policy experience, I contrived a way for it to be implicitly mentioned. I delved into the speeches and writings of all the world statesmen Nixon had met in his world travels—Churchill, Adenauer, de Gaulle, de Gasperi, Tito, and Nehru.

For example, Nixon would say, "I remember meeting Prime Minister Nehru in New Delhi, and one of his favorite sayings was, 'What the world needs is a generation of peace.' (Mind you, I didn't expressly say that Nixon heard Nehru utter those words.) In that regard, I remember Ted Sorensen saying that in the 1960 campaign when Kennedy went to Texas, the candidate told him to come up with some Irish Catholics who had died at the Alamo. Unfortunately, those with Irish names were all Protestants. So Sorensen wrote, "When Jim Brady, Pat Sullivan, and Jack Kelley died at the Alamo, no one asked them whether they were Catholics."

Names have power in Washington. If Potomac Fever is a disease endemic to Washington, one of its symptoms is name dropping.

I remember being at a Georgetown dinner party in the late 1950s. One of the guests was pontificating on his experience in the councils of power. "As I told Dean [Acheson]..." or "Of course, Clark Clifford had my memorandum..."

As we sipped our after-dinner drinks, the host excused himself and returned with a whisk broom and dustpan. The self-appointed counselor to the powerful stopped in the midst of his account of his stint in the State Department and said, "Bob, what are you doing?"

"Oh, don't mind me," he said. "I'm just sweeping up the dropped names."

Alice Roosevelt Longworth once told me at her house on Massachusetts Avenue off Dupont Circle, "James, Washington is power, then the access to power, and finally the illusion of access to power."

You only have to be a minor cog in Washington to glean this truth. If a fetching blonde were to be talking to a Tom Cruise look-alike at a Washington cocktail party and a myopic gnome was suddenly introduced to her as "Kissinger's man on Asia" or "Nixon's favorite professor," she would drop the Cruise clone in a moment.

When I was in law school, a secretary I had known (ironically, through the Young Republicans), was transferred from the Pentagon to JFK's White House. I encountered her on the street sometime after her move.

"James, I'm working my tail off for the same salary," she began. "I knew there would be long hours, but I thought there'd be some glamour and excitement. I haven't had a date in a month of Sundays."

"Amy, you know where the White House pool is?"

"Yes."

"And you know that powder room right next to it?"

"Uh huh."

"Well, at your morning coffee break go to that Ladies Room. Fill the basin full of water. Dunk your head. Don't dry it, shake it, and go back to your office, and give me a call in a couple of weeks."

Weeks later she called. "My hair's a mess, but I've had dates with a cultural attaché at the French embassy, a colonel in the Pentagon, and a young congressman. They keep asking me about the trade bill, the tax bill, and what the president's thinking. Well, if I see the president, it's on TV."

"Amy," I replied, "you know the president swims every day."

"Yes."

"He swims nude."

"Yes."

"Jackie never goes there, and not all his companions are male."

"Jamie—you've hurt my reputation."

"No, Amy, I've helped it."

The staffer's secret in the ascent to power is adulation. In Washington, flattery drives out truth. It's like Gresham's Law in Economics, in which bad coins drive out good ones. Inflated paeans of praise to the boss prevail over the gold coin of truth. For survival in the cut-throat world of Washington politics, blarney might count more than brains.

Someone with a surplus of both was Henry Kissinger. A devotee of Otto van Bismarck, he also admired the Iron Chancellor's contemporary in European statecraft, Benjamin Disraeli. The British statesman once revealed his secret in dealing with Queen Victoria. "When dealing with Her Majesty, I lay it on with a trowel."

Kissinger would tell Nixon that he was "the greatest president in history," while privately denigrating Nixon to his staff. Kissinger, with his heavy German accent, could fit Churchill's dictum: "The Hun is either at your throat or at your feet."

On one occasion, I was asked to craft a toast to Prime Minister Pierre Trudeau of Canada, who was to be a guest at a White House State Dinner. I called a Canadian friend, who sent me Trudeau's doctoral thesis at the University of Montreal. In it was his description of a former Canadian leader, Sir Wilfred Laurier. "A leader must not only know how to swim upstream, but when."

In my drafted remarks, I was to have Nixon say, "The head of one of our great Western democracies once defined leadership in this way…," concealing until the end that the writer had been Trudeau himself as a student.

Kissinger come barging into my office, shouting, "Humes, did you write this piece of human excrement…?"

I had not been told that what Kissinger wanted in the toast was a buildup of Canadian–American ties and a brush-off of Trudeau, whose leftist policies Nixon and Kissinger despised.

Kissinger's tirades against underlings who couldn't fight back was his trademark. Even worse, he would steal their ideas and shamelessly claim the credit.

Early in the Nixon presidency, I advanced the idea that the president honor artist Andrew Wyeth with a dinner. On the Shakespeare Quadricentennial Commission, on which I had served with him, Wyeth had told me he admired Nixon. Since I knew that Nixon liked his work, I thought that a dinner showcasing his paintings at the White House would help both the president and the painter.

Pianists and singers had entertained at the White House previously, but never had an artist been the occasion for a dinner.

Kissinger scratched my name off the memo and then pushed it as his own idea. I was even blocked from going to the dinner, though at the last minute I managed to wangle an invitation through Lucy Winchester, the White House social secretary. (The dinner, I like to think, boosted the popularity of Wyeth and led to the building of the Brandywine Museum in Chadds Ford, Pennsylvania.)

If privately Kissinger could at times be a rat, publicly he was a lion—one of our greatest secretaries of state. As an aide, I can say that his briefings after a foreign mission were mesmerizing, replete with charm, wit, and historical allusion.

Still, a Kissinger aide said to me after he had left the White House: "Kissinger could give lessons to Nixon in neurotic paranoia."

In 1970, I had an interview with Al Haig, then a colonel on Kissinger's National Security Staff. Haig, in coat and tie, was talking to me, when Kissinger, coatless, interrupted in his guttural bass.

"Al, may I speak to you for a second?"

Haig rose with a salute.

"Yes, Doctor."

That told me a lot about both men.

Of course, I was informed later that Haig, when he was secretary of state under Reagan, would rise saluting, even when it was only a phone call from the president!

The press made much of the Teutonic flavor of the White House. The names of Haldeman, Ehrlichman, as well as the brief experiment of ceremonial uniforms out of a Viennese operetta, exaggerated the impression.

When I left the White House for the State Department, Haldeman gave me a gift at my farewell party. It was two bottles of white, nonalcoholic grape juice from Germany. The fact that it was German and without spirits might be interpreted as a tangible metaphor for the humorless Haldeman.

Haldeman and Ehrlichman were Christian Scientists who did not drink. Neither did many of the Mormons who peopled the White House staff. Still, I found that in IQ and intellectual stimulation, the Nixon White House made the Ford White House staff seem like a drove of dullards and drones.

In the Nixon White House mess, you encountered special assistants like Henry Kissinger, Pat Moynihan, Arthur Burns, Herb Stein, and Jean Mayer (later president of Tufts). If the Ford staff had a lot of congressional hacks, there was a heap of Harvard in the Nixon White House.

And if Haldeman was in some ways a humorless traffic controller, he served the purpose for Nixon. Nixon preferred dealing with paper rather than people. Strangely, he was an introvert in an extrovert's profession. Nixon used Haldeman not only to control the influx of paper, but also as insulation. Haldeman, like a modern computer, could give Nixon a readout on any issue or problem—he would brief Nixon on the key politicians, players, and interest blocs standing in the way of certain proposals. Nixon disdained the small talk schmoozing that his predecessor LBJ reveled in. Meetings with groups in the White House were more symbolic than substantive. Since he already knew the positions of antiwar critics or civil rights activists, he begrudged the time given to those meetings held for "show" purposes because they took away time needed for reflection and thinking.

Haldeman was not an adviser to the president so much as a neutral processor. He also recognized that Nixon needed an ear in which to let off steam and that not all his private fulminations should be translated to fiats. Haldeman was a functionary, albeit a powerful one, but not a social intimate of the president.

Nixon's close friends outside his family were old supporters like Elmer Bobst and Bob Apbanalp. A friend is someone you can relax with, someone with whom you can talk without any pretense or guarded manner: that was Bebe Rebozo. Bebe, a Floridian of Cuban extraction, knew the secret of quiet companionship.

A White House aide, in describing the Rebozo friendship, said to me, "Jamie, Bebe is the successor to Checkers."

"You think that's criticism of Bebe," I replied. "I'd call it a compliment! The human race has a lot to learn from the canine. Who doesn't like good companionship and total loyalty without demands?"

Bebe would spend hours with Nixon, sometimes without a word. When conversation did ensue, Nixon would initiate it.

That doesn't mean Nixon was cold. Of all the five presidents I have worked with, he was the warmest in a working relationship and the most considerate of one's needs.

If I had to work on a weekend, Nixon would ask, "Jamie, would Dianne and the girls like to go to Camp David?" Perhaps it was that Nixon had a warm spot for my wife. I was always "the guy who married Dianne," not the reverse.

The stiff, awkward Nixon was the public Nixon seen in receptions and public meetings. Some have told me that the Nixon with the most winning personality, Julie excepted, was his brother, Harold. He was the mother's favorite. He died on her birthday at age nineteen, and Hannah Nixon would never again let her birthday be celebrated.

Nixon told Jonathan Aitken (a British MP and biographer of Nixon) that the happy-go-lucky hero of *Carousel* reminded him of Harold. In high school and college, Nixon was the nerd that the smooth set disdained. Yet, by outworking them all, he would outdistance them. He once told me, "Jamie, it doesn't take brains to get top grades in law school—it takes an iron butt to stick to the books."

Still, Nixon tried hard to be one of the boys. One way was his mastery of baseball and football trivia.

Yet, his attempt to make small talk sometimes had bizarre results. In 1972 in Detroit, one of the cars in a presidential motorcade ran over a policeman. Nixon went back to talk to the man lying on the curb. Nixon looked down and said, "Officer, how do you like the job?"

Nixon would never be one of the boys. He might invite Elvis Presley to the White House and fête country western singers, but he preferred classical music. He might despise the academic elite for their ideological blinkers, but he shared their habit of academic discipline. Nixon was an intellectual and a scholar. He was no gladhander. He was a loner in a hail-fellow-well-met world.

A European wrote that Americans worship their automobile. If so, Nixon was an agnostic. Machinery and mechanics not only bored him but also were beyond him.

I remember one time riding on a train with him. "Get me some pain killers, please," he said to an aide. Aspirin was brought. Afterward, I looked at the child-proof bottle cap and could see his teethmarks. The picture of the president of the United States trying to open the bottle by using his teeth is comic commentary on his lack of physical dexterity. I sympathize and understand because I lack the same skills. Like Nixon, I write this book on yellow legal pads. The typewriter—much less the word processor—is beyond my skills.

Tom Wicker, who reviled Nixon in the seventies, wrote a somewhat sympathetic biography of him in the nineties entitled *One of Us*. He meant it in the sense that Nixon embodied all the hopes, fears, and anxieties of the average Joe as he pursued the American dream of success.

Nixon, through speechwriter Ray Price, coined the phrase that described those average Americans—"Silent Majority."

The Silent Majority speech of November 1969 ranks along with his Checkers speech as one of the most telling speeches of his career. Both had the impact of reversing the tide of public opinion.

The Nixon White House was unprepared for the October march in Washington by war protestors that year—but it was ready for the November demonstrations.

In the Policy Council, we were asked for our ideas. Some suggested a day of prayer, others a preemptive strike. Nixon chose the latter. He commissioned Pat Buchanan to draft two speeches for Vice President Agnew—the first attacking the press, and the second the electronic media. If Ray Price was the golden retriever of the writers who conjured up "the lilt of a driving dream," Pat was the Doberman pinscher, the attack dog. Actually, Agnew was reluctant to be the press-baiter, but Nixon was adamant. He remembered his role of playing the partisan heavy for the publicly benign Ike.

If the press made Agnew a liability in the 1968 campaign, he had proved himself a winner in mobilizing middle America. At a Heritage meeting I attended at the White House in October (an assembly of Italian, Greek, and other Eastern European ethnics), the vice president drew more cheers than the president. Agnew's widely reported address weeks before denouncing "the effete corps of intellectual snobs" had struck a resonant chord in middle America.

That speech, curiously, was written by a Lindsay Republican, Cindy Rosenwald. She had come to work for Republican Agnew when he was fighting George ("My home is my castle") Mahoney, a George Wallace Democrat for the Maryland governorship.

Agnew's "effete snob" talk was delivered several times to Republican audiences in the North, but it aroused national coverage only when Agnew delivered it in New Orleans. That's when the *New York*

Times and *Washington Post* sent journalists to report on Nixon's southern strategy. Their reports hit a raw nerve.

Buchanan, in his first draft for Vice President Agnew's "effete snobs" speech, even quoted his own boyhood heroes, Douglas MacArthur and Joe McCarthy.

My cross-quotesmanship suggestion to him of citing what Theodore White and Dave Broder had said in their columns about "the monolithic nature of the Eastern press" was dismissed.

I got to know Theodore White in the 1964 campaign when he was covering Bill Scranton. One Sunday in New York, he took me to Fraunce's Tavern. (This restaurant, near Wall Street, is the city's oldest and the site where Washington bid farewell to his officers.)

This gnome of a man could detach himself from the liberal mindset of most national reporters. "Jamie, our values, preferences, and habits may be as parochial as the Mormons. We are a narrow group who feel as superior in our worldliness as the Mormons do in their godliness."

In November, the press suddenly found itself on the defensive. The one-two punch of Nixon's appeal to the silent majority and Agnew's attack on the bias of the national press and television made the media temporarily sheath their claws. Then, too, Nixon's first withdrawal of American troops from Vietnam silenced his critics, for a time.

The Nixon pledge in the campaign of 1968 that he had a "solution to Vietnam" has been denounced as a cynical election ploy. Actually, he had spelled out his plan, "to Vietnamize the War," to a few of his friends. The November speech was the first step in carrying that out.

Following the speech, we in the White House staff were conscripted to call every governor—Democrat as well as Republican—to issue words supporting our American boys on November 11, Veterans Day.

The massive November antiwar demonstration fizzled, not only figuratively but literally. The press muted its coverage of a protest whose numbers dwindled under sheets of rain. One White House staffer told me of his plan to seed the clouds for that November day. Whether he actually involved the Pentagon in this scheme is not known, but if so, Nixon never knew about it. Yet, it did rain buckets in Washington—but not across the Potomac in Virginia!

That rainy day was the first time I saw John Kerry, the Vietnam veteran and future U.S. senator. Dressed in his camouflage garb, he attended a black-tie Georgetown dinner dance where he made the post-debutante hearts flutter. He did not spend the torrential night in the muddy Ellipse with his co-demonstrators but in the Georgetown house of his grandmother.

Nixon—not Kerry and his fellow protestors—won the psychological offensive that November. Approval ratings of Nixon's policies climbed to over 70 percent. Middle America sided with the president.

Today, it is never mentioned that over 70 percent of the college youth voted for Nixon against McGovern in 1972. In 1970, my cousin John Humes, himself a Princeton graduate and ambassador to Austria, hosted the president when he came to Vienna for the SALT talks conference.

John Humes said, "Mr. President, it's not the Ivy League but the Poison Ivy League." Nixon laughed, "You got it right, John."

But if Princeton, Yale, and Harvard students had the louder voice, those working-class families that went to the state universities and the night schools outvoted them.

In the era of Ben Hecht's play *Front Page,* the big city reporters were people from the streets of the big cities, not from the suburbs; they came out from high schools, not St. Paul's and Andover. The new elite of the media barely disguise their scorn for working-class beliefs like religion and patriotism, which they ridicule as Archie Bunker values.

But to Nixon, these people were the Silent Majority. The rise of Nixon to the presidency embodied their dreams.

On my lecture tours, I have often talked about "a president who, despite his skills and triumphs in foreign policies, found himself mired in domestic scandal. This president," I go on to say, "would leave the White House with the lowest approval rating in this century. His attorney-general was indicted. Those politically close to him in the White House or elsewhere were charged with malfeasance in office. A bill of impeachment against him was introduced in the House." And then, after a pause, I like to say, "I'm talking about Harry Truman."

"Mr. President," I said to former President Nixon as I walked with him on San Clemente Beach in the summer of 1975, "people remember Truman for the Marshall Plan and Truman Doctrine. But they forget that when he left Washington in 1953 his approval rating was 18 percent—two below yours last year. They forget the mink coats and refrigerators scandals involving the White House and the IRS in 1950 or that his attorney-general, McGranery, was indicted.

"Mr. Nixon," I concluded, "foreign policy triumphs are writ large in the pages of history books, and that will come to be your lasting legacy."

The former president, dressed in maroon blazer, knit tie, and polished Gucci loafers, shook his head ruefully.

I had been doing some talk show appearances for my book *Podium Humor* in Los Angeles and decided to drive down one August Saturday morning to have lunch with the former president.

On the way down, my mind turned back to my research on presidential memoirs. The president-elect in December 1968 had asked to read my research notes. (Those of Ulysses Grant, by the way, are the best.)

I suggested to Nixon that he write more than a day-by-day chronicle of his public career accomplishments—that he include observations on the presidency and government in order to guide future politicians and students.

I had notes of what de Tocqueville in *American Democracy*, James Bryce in *American Commonwealth*, Woodrow Wilson in *Congressional Government*, and others had to say about the presidency, so that he could reinforce or challenge their conclusions. That is what I mainly talked about to Nixon that afternoon—because I wanted to avoid Watergate.

As he walked me out to my car, I told him I would call his writer about the citations I had collected from presidential memoirs and political writings.

"No, Jamie," he said. "We've always been friends. Here's my number, call me."

As I got into the car, the former president stooped and in a cracked voice said, "Jamie, I'm sorry if I let you down."

I was shaken. My first stop after leaving his house was the San Clemente Inn for a couple of martinis.

In the 1980s, I went on three trips for the State Department in Asia and Latin America, where I addressed universities, business councils, and seminars on U.S. government and foreign policy. The president who drew the most interest and questions was Nixon. To the educated and professional classes, he was the most admired. Of course, you have to remember that foreigners see U.S. presidents through the prism of foreign policy, and Nixon, in that light, was deservedly the most highly esteemed.

It only confirmed what had been my own experience in my many trips to Britain. That was why I suggested to Nixon in San Clemente that he begin his emergence from exile by speaking at Oxford, which he later did with the help of Jonathan Aitken, his future biographer, now reckoned to be a future leader of the Tory Party, who gave Nixon the same advice.

John Kennedy, with his Hollywood glamour, was naturally the darling of those who read the tabloids, but Nixon fascinated the people who read the foreign policy quarterly and opinion pieces. If I was having drinks at London's Carlton Club or at Kowloon's Peninsula Hotel, eventually someone would say, "Nixon was so bright—how could he get involved in something so stupid as Watergate?"

Well, brains has nothing to do with it. I know a lawyer who had a Mensa IQ and was a former editor of his law review, and he left his wife to marry the *au pair* girl!

In answering, I always begin by telling that my friend Bob Smith, former chief counsel of the Government Operations Committee under Sam Ervin, predicted that Nixon would be impeached on Inauguration Day of 1969! He even bet me 10 to 1 odds.

Smith showed me a list of the Republican members of the House Judiciary Committee who had voted for the impeachment of Justice Abe Fortas in 1967.

"Jamie," he argued, "let Nixon make one mistake, and he's gone! Don't think the Judiciary Committee votes like judges—it's partisan and political. And there is, under the surface, an ugly mood in Congress that's fed up with an executive branch that from FDR to LBJ has pushed presidential powers beyond the constitutional limit.

"Look at Roosevelt and the Japanese internment," he continued. "The IRS at Kennedy's order descended on the U.S. Steel executives who opposed him, Johnson's deceived on the Gulf of Tonkin affair—why, it's the same mood Congress was in after the Civil War, World War I, and World War II. A partisan Congress went after the president, a president in the other party."

I thought about that in the summer of 1969 when LBJ's former press secretary, George Reedy, wrote the book *Twilight of the Presidency*. He anticipated Watergate by saying that an expanding White House staff under Johnson planted the seeds for abuse of power. I sent a memorandum to President Nixon underlying passages of the book.

In a nutshell, the gravamen of the case against the president was his deception about the coverup. Previous presidents have lied, but Nixon is the only one to pay such a heavy cost. As Senator Sam Ervin later concluded, Nixon had no knowledge before the fact of the break-in at the Democratic National Committee Headquarters, but he did abet in concealing White House involvement.

One question that I am frequently asked is, "Why didn't he

destroy the tapes?" One possible reason came from Bob Haldeman after he left the White House in 1974. Haldeman said that he thought the CIA had copies. Alex Butterfield, a holdover from the LBJ White House, had set up the Oval Office taping system, and he later revealed the operation to Senator Ervin to save himself from indictment. Butterfield, Haldeman suspected, was a conduit to the CIA since he handled liaison work with the Agency in the White House. The CIA was staffed by the Ivy League types who never liked the bourgeois Nixon. They also thought themselves above government and even the law. They feared Nixon, as chief executive, would use his constitutional powers to look into their unsupervised activities. They might have wanted their own copy of the tapes as leverage against Nixon. John Ehrlichman, in his *roman à clef* novel after he left the White House, pushed the same theory.

The other question is: "Why didn't he wield some damage control and let the whole story come out in 1972? It wouldn't have mattered in the election."

My answer is that the breaking developments in the Watergate burglary, the people involved, and the connections to the Nixon campaign were reported to Nixon incrementally by the top White House aides, who gave each briefing the right spin to insulate themselves from their own involvement and accountability.

It reminds me of a CEO with an indulgent wife, parents of a wayward son. To protect the son, the wife said to the busy executive, "Junior had an accident last night, but everything's okay."

Weeks later she tells him, "Junior was drinking."

A month later, "Well, actually a man was hit."

Then later, "He didn't report it to the police."

And finally, "Well, the man died."

The business executive so engrossed in the affairs of the company didn't want to know about the son. Psychologically, avoidance was easier. When everything did come out, it was a scandal that quick and early action could have forestalled.

Well, Nixon was involved with China and didn't want to know about the operations in CREEP, and he paid the price of later protecting the White House staff who had failed to deliver all the facts at the first news of the arrest.

And then, too, I remember an incident in October 1960. The Nixon campaign office was broken into and files stolen. We called a press conference. The few reporters who came treated it as political tricks that were part of the game. In fact, they saluted the Kennedy team for pulling it off.

Watergate was like a minor infection that was left to fester. The hostile media turned their glare on the boil to make it look like cancer of the whole body.

Some of the other press reports of so-called Watergates were typical cases of presidential pressure on bureaucrats, who then leaked to the press to ingratiate themselves with the congressional chairmen who funded their agencies. Well, the president has the right to lean on bureaucrats. He is, after all, the chief executive.

One question I am *always* asked is "Who was Deep Throat?" The short answer, I believe, is Dave Gergen. At least, he was the major leak from the White House. His name was given to me by at least two aides who served in the Nixon White House at that time. They also say that Nixon nodded assent when they later told this to the former president. The argument against it is that his position was not important enough for him to be privy to high-level conferences. Yet, Gergen sat in every day for Ray Price at the 8:00 A.M. White House staff meeting of top aides called by Chief of Staff Haldeman. Price, who had succeeded Jim Keogh as head of the speechwriters, was not an early riser since he often worked into the early morning hours.

The leaking was not done in a garage but by telephone. Woodward, who had worked with Gergen on the *Yale Record*, would call Gergen at the office. Gergen would not speak, according to witnesses who often observed this ritual. He would be silent for long stretches, sometimes punctuating the silence with a soft no. The silence would indicate an assent to what Woodward was saying on the other end. A "no" would signal that Woodward had bad information.

That said, however, the whole "Deep Throat" story has always struck me as something of a theatrical exaggeration. It was a sensational name (after the porno film of that title) devised by Woodward and Bernstein to enable them to slip their story by *Washington Post* editor, Ben Bradley. Journalistic rules prevent reporting an account that is quoted from an unnamed source, the exception to the rule being if parts of the story can be corroborated by several named sources.

Woodward and Bernstein tried to shape and fit the various pieces into one convincing and coherent account. Then they imputed the entire account to a single supposed "Deep Throat," and to substantiate it, they pointed to verification by the sources they could identify by name.

One "tyranny" the media still love to point to with horror is the so-called "Enemies List." It all began when Nixon exploded when some Hollywood actress, a prominent Nixon-hater, was invited to a White House dinner. The Nixon gripe was grist for John Dean's mill.

John Dean, who plotted the Watergate break-in for his own self-interest, also had a hand in the Enemies List.

With his sly intrigues and servile manner, Dean was the combination of an Iago and a Uriah Heep. Dean made a list of those in Hollywood, the press, and academic circles whom everyone knew were no fans of Nixon.

Actually, presidents have long exercised their whims in dinner invitations. President Carter once crossed off Governor Jerry Brown from the list of those who were to attend a banquet for the president of Mexico, although the California governor is always included as a matter of protocol.

By the way, when I heard of the list, I put in the name of a liberal journalist friend that I knew would never get invited to a state dinner anyway. He still dines out on virtue of being a member of the list and never fails to pick up the tab when we meet for drinks.

De Tocqueville once wrote that every political issue in America is a constitutional issue. That was true with Andrew Johnson in 1866 and with Truman (the seizure of the steel mills, etc.) in 1950. Watergate was, in effect, an American version of a British failure of a confidence vote.

Chapter Twelve

NIXON DIPLOMAT

Turn him to any cause of policy,
The Guardian knot of it he will unloose
familiar as his garter.
HENRY V

t a Christmas party at Vice President Nixon's home on Forest Lane, Washington, I heard Nixon say to a group of us, "Some day, I'll go to China."

Stupidly, I said, "You mean Formosa?" (the island off Taiwan to which the Republic of China Nationalist supporters of Chiang Kai-shek, the generalissimo, had fled).

"No," he replied, "When I said China, I meant China—Mainland China."

His reply triggered memories of an earlier time I overheard Nixon in a conversation with an assistant, Agnes Waldron. "The generalissimo isn't all that bright; the real brains in the family is his wife."

A few years back, I enjoyed posing this teaser at dinner parties. I would say, "I recently [1993] introduced the most powerful figure in World War II that is still alive." Some offered the names of Jimmy Doolittle (he died in 1992) or Omar Bradley (he died in 1982).

After their wrong guesses, I would say, "Madame Chiang Kai-shek." This was October 1993 at the National Arts Club. The ninety-one-year-old lady was driven in from her Westchester County nursing home. She left Taiwan when her stepson succeeded his father in 1977. The tiny, frail woman just managed to negotiate her steps to the head table without assistance. But in conversation, her mind seemed not in the least diminished by age.

Actually, the generalissimo's wife was far more influential in diplomacy and politics than her fellow Wellesley graduate, Hillary Clinton.

In the 1950s, the foremost champion of Chiang Kai-shek was the senior senator from California, William Knowland. The press jokingly referred to him as "the Senator from Formosa." Those who assumed that the views of the junior senator from California, Richard Nixon, were in lockstep with Knowland were mistaken.

The liberal press, which stereotyped Nixon as the politician who built a career on being an anticommunist, did not pick up on Nixon's article in *Foreign Affairs* in the spring of 1967 entitled "What's After Vietnam?" The article, drafted in 1966, warned against excluding "Mainland China from the world community."

The overture to China early in the Nixon administration was solely a Nixon idea. Kissinger's interest was Europe, and his knowledge of Asia only marginally exceeded that of the moon. In fact, Kissinger didn't want to go to China at all. At one point he cried to Fritz Kramer, an anti-Hitler German émigré who taught Kissinger everything he knew about foreign policy, that going to China would be the end of his career. Kramer replied that sometimes you have to pick the less powerful of the two enemies. When Kissinger went to Nixon and said that he didn't want to go, Nixon said, "That's all right, I'll send Bill Rogers." Needless to say, Kissinger went to China.

Yet Nixon's idea of opening relations with China was not based on romantic sentiment or idealistic principle; it was the *realpolitik* of a far-seeing statesman. Early in his administration, Nixon spurned feelers for a summit with the Soviet Union. He wanted to come to such a meeting with the cards stacked in his favor.

Nixon, a seasoned poker player who turned his meager naval

salary into a small nestegg in his ship days in the South Pacific, once said to a group of us in an allusion to stud poker, "I wanted a couple of aces showing when I opened the bidding with the Soviets."

One of those aces would be access to Mainland China, the estranged partner of the Sino-Soviet communist bloc. Another would be an Anti-Ballistic Missile (ABM) defense set up in America.

The ABM was passed by only one vote in the Senate. To politicians who privately questioned whether the system would actually repel a nuclear missile, Nixon reportedly replied, "The Russians don't know whether it will work, but they won't dare find out the hard way. You see, the ABM is another face card showing when you're across the table in treaty negotiations."

China watchers in the State Department and Sinologists at Harvard and Georgetown advised Nixon that no opening to China could take place until America pulled out of Vietnam.

Nixon scoffed at their counsel. He knew Vietnam was the client of the Soviet Union and that Mao's support of the Ho Chi Minh was nominal and minimal. Why would they want their ancient border enemy, Russia, to expand its influence on their southern flank in Indochina?

I had confirmation of this in March 1970. I was visiting my cousin, John Humes, who, as I said, was our ambassador in Austria. One night at the Bristol Hotel, I ran into an English-speaking Red Chinese delegation who were nursing their drinks. They bought me a drink, even though the United States at that time still recognized Taiwan as "China."

I offered them some cigars I had with me. "But these are Cuban," one of them said. "You do not recognize them."

"Well," I said, "we don't recognize you either but I can enjoy your company."

Perhaps they thought the reply of this low-ranking Nixon aide was replete with cryptic meaning, because they bent my ear for an hour with warnings for the United States. Not once did the subject of Vietnam come up. What they feared was our ongoing SALT talks in Vienna with the Soviets, whom they warned me not to trust.

While we were staying at the embassy residence, their counsel to distrust the Soviets was reinforced. In the "chicken coop," the Plexiglas room-within-a-room on top of the embassy, a siren went off. This was the bug-proof room where French, British, Italians, and Americans would meet to discuss strategy. The alarm meant that everyone in attendance had to undergo a strip search. The bug was found in a British diplomat's shoe. He had taken it to be resoled a week before!

Of course, my visit to Vienna was purely social. Yet, strangely, the Soviets knew I was coming even before I called Jean Humes, John's wife, to give the date of our arrival. At a dinner at the French Embassy weeks before, the Soviet ambassador said to Jean:

"Madame Ambassador, I understand your cousin is coming in two weeks to visit you."

I had informed only a few in the State Department of my visit, but word had leaked out to the Soviets. John Humes was convinced that the Soviets thought I was hand-carrying a special message to our disarmament team.

It reminds me of a comment Vice President Nixon made to a group of us after a three-hour meeting with Anatole Mikoyan in Washington in 1958. (The visit of the high-ranking Soviet to Washington was the first stop in a reciprocal exchange that would send the vice president to Moscow a year later.) Nixon was amazed at some of the criticisms Mikoyan leveled at the Soviet system: the failure of collectivization and the economic plan, and the admission that they were initiating some financial incentive programs to stimulate production and family farms. Nixon wanted to get Mikoyan's statements in writing so that his own translator could make up a transcript. On receiving it, he found that the critical passages had been deleted.

When he reported this to John Foster Dulles, Dulles said, "Dick, we have communists in the State Department. But it won't help you to say so."

Visiting communist countries makes you even more paranoid. A couple of years ago, my wife and I were staying at the National Hotel in Moscow (what John Gunther in *Inside Europe* called the "St. Regis of Russia"). I had managed to wedge my ample frame into the room's tiny bathtub only to find that the soap bar was not much larger than a quarter piece. I roared, "You would think that in this communist utopia where cleanliness ranks second only to equality there would be soap!" A few minutes later a maid rushed in with a bar of soap.

One advantage of a police state is that the service can be ultra-sensitive to your wishes and words. After I dried myself, I felt a lump in the carpet under my feet. I pulled the carpet back. There "it" was. With my Swiss knife, I started to unscrew the little gizmo. When I finished, I heard a resounding crash beneath me. I had undone the support that held the chandelier in the room below!

But it's better to be red with embarrassment than blackmailed by Reds. One afternoon, while my wife was being entertained at a concert, I was taken in hand by my Intourist guide. Olga looked like a Dolly Parton—just as petite and just as large. In the Kremlin, she took me past an array of models of former czarinas, who displayed figures almost as dramatic as hers.

"Dr. Humes," she said, "you do not find these women attractive?"

"No, why do you say that?"

"Why, in the pictures of your fashion magazines it looks like the women here" and she motioned to her chest "have them cut off."

After a moment she looked me in the face and said, "Then you find me not unattractive?"

I nodded nervously.

When we got back to the hotel, she said, "Couldn't we have a drink in your room?"

I'd like to think it was my physical appeal, but know it was my presidential connections. Fidelity was not the only reason I said, "Olga, you will excuse me—I have a terrible headache."

That was the summer of 1972. I had just left the Nixon administration and arranged a trip to Moscow. The Soviets threw out a red carpet for me because it was the height of detente. Nixon reigned triumphant as the world leader who had just completed a successful summit with Brezhnev (not to mention his opening up relations with China earlier in January). I had a four-hour vodka-laced lunch at the American Institute with George Abatov and Anatole Gromyko, discussing American politics. One item I learned was that the Americanologists there always read the right-hand story of the *Wall Street Journal* as the truest glimpse of Main Street American life.

Another day, I was the guest of honor at a luncheon hosted by Ed Stevens, the Moscow correspondent of *Newsday*. On that sweltering day of over 100 degrees, Stevens and his Russian-born wife greeted many of the press and TV personalities who attended the well-served fête. Steven's wife, Olga, the rumor went, was a Cossack who had disquised herself as a man in order to attend a Russian military school.

At the luncheon, Stevens delivered a fulsome toast to me and the statesmanship of Richard Nixon. Afterward, I heard John Chancellor question him: "You just praised Nixon—I remember you once called him a fascist henchman of Joe McCarthy."

Stevens smiled. "He's matured. He's a world leader today."

Afterward, I told Chancellor, "You know why Stevens liked Nixon in the election over McGovern? He's following the party line—he's a communist."

My observation triggered contempt from some of the newsmen present.

"You Republicans see Reds under every bed," someone inevitably remarked.

"Look," I replied, "only an American with tight connections to the Kremlin would have an AP news ticker in his house. He's the only foreigner to have his own house, not an apartment, and he even has servants."

"So what does that prove?" said Chancellor.

"Well, consider this. He was active for Henry Wallace for president against Truman in 1948 and for Nixon against McGovern this year. I spent last afternoon with Gromyko's son; they're for Nixon, they can deal with him, they despise bourgeois liberals like McGovern. Why else would he make me a guest of honor?"

My opinion was confirmed in 1994 when newly revealed communist records revealed that Stevens had been on the party payroll for twenty years.

If the Russians respected Nixon, the Chinese revered him. In 1985, a decade or more after I left government, I made some speeches in Beijing and Shanghai on a visit arranged by USIA (the U.S. Information Agency). For the Chinese communists, Nixon was the leader who reached out to shake Chou-En Lai's hand in 1972, erasing the refused handshake by Secretary of State Dulles in Geneva in 1954.

For the Chinese, Nixon was a living link to the dead Mao.

At a reception given me by a counsellor in our embassy in Beijing, the American staff was startled by the surprise visit of a young Chinese woman, Nancy Twan. She had been Mao's English interpreter and had grown up in Brooklyn, the daughter of a Red Chinese UN diplomat. Nancy stayed only briefly. She wanted me to let former President Nixon know she was still alive.

Afterward, my American hosts told me that for years she had dropped out of sight. They had figured that, like others in the Mao entourage, she was in prison or worse.

But if, as a former Nixon speechwriter, I was accorded a warm reception by my Chinese hosts, surveillance was not relaxed.

One evening I called a cab outside my hotel to go to the Chinese Wall, one of Beijing's top restaurants. While I was eating my Peking duck, which I thought appropriate—it was the worst Peking Duck

I ever had—I got a call from a Chinese official. Since I hadn't made a reservation, the Chinese must have had me followed.

In the spring of 1970, I was kicked upstairs to the State Department as director of the Office of Policy and Plans in Public Affairs. I went as deputy to astronaut Michael Collins because it was thought the Apollo XI lunar landing hero would be the ideal spokesman to explain our foreign policy to civic and college audiences.

As his deputy, I would help draft speeches for the newly appointed assistant secretary of state and give some speeches in my own right. As a speechwriter, I helped coin the Nixon administration's hallmark phrase "Let us move from the era of confrontation to the era of negotiation."

Shortly after the Bay of Pigs in 1961, I saw Nixon, who had called on President Kennedy at his invitation. He told us that Kennedy seemed shaken by the incident. Nixon then reported former President Eisenhower's reaction. "Dick, for U.S. military intervention, you need four conditions: First, congressional support. Second, the occupation must be limited in time, or you will loose the support of pubic opinion. Third, there must be a viable leader with a broad popular backing to succeed the ousted dictator. And finally, whatever troops you need, take ten times more."

In Cuba, Eisenhower said, he put a hold on the contingency plan for lack of the right successor to Castro. But if he had gone into Cuba, he would not have done a half-assed job without air support.

That was the basis of Nixon's "no more Vietnam." In Guam, he pledged what Kissinger called "the Nixon Doctrine"—no more would U.S. troops be dispatched to an Asian nation to sustain a country's fight against a communist insurgency—only military and economic aid would be sent. In talks to college audiences, I would say something along the lines of:

> Look, there is a difference between the Nixon
> administration and the previous Johnson administration.

They kept sending more American boys in; we have
started pulling them out. There's another big turn-
around that distinguishes this administration. For the
first time since 1942, the government is spending more
on social problems and projects than on defense.

I would then speak of the peace initiatives made in the Mideast
and the disarmament talks, i.e., Nixon's analogy that when you mow
the lawn, you begin at the outer edge and move to the center. So, I
said, Nixon, in his dealings with the Soviets, has started on the
peripheral problems first—fishing and trade disputes—and is working his way to the core problems such as nuclear disarmament.

It was persuasive to the audiences of trade associations and civic
clubs. It was a harder sell to campuses, particularly in the midst of
Vietnik protestors.

One ploy I developed for the hecklers in this Age of Aquarius was
to ask the taunters, with a smile, "What's your sign?"

If someone said, "Aries," the ram, I would answer, "No wonder
you try to butt in."

To a "Pisces," the fish—"No wonder your argument's all wet."

To a "Taurus," the bull—"I should have known you're so full of
BS."

I tried to do it with a smile and chuckle—never answer anger
with anger. At one university I was invited to, it couldn't work. Harvard informed me that for reasons of safety they disallowed a live
appearance. I could, however, send a recording of my talk.

So much for the liberal arts, which I thought meant competition
of ideas. But what could you expect of a college that refused to invite
back former Harvard professor Dr. Henry Kissinger (who had been
on leave), but would extend invitations to far-out people like Angela
Davis and Herbert Marcuse?

I got my revenge when my good friend, John Le Boutillier, wrote
of his experiences with the left-minded set at Cambridge. I

suggested as his title *Harvard Hates America,* and he dedicated the book to me.

In some ways, my State Department experience was a disappointment. I discovered that diplomats were generally bureaucrats with passports. The problem is that any recommended course of foreign policy action is shipwrecked in the three Cs—Conference, Consensus, and CYA (cover your ass).

One State Department colleague laughingly said, "Jamie, sometimes it works out that inaction is the best policy." As an example, he pointed to a crisis that had emerged in a third world country in February of 1958. A blizzard forced the State Department to shut down. There were two snow days, followed by a long presidential weekend. When they got back to work on Tuesday, the crisis had solved itself. Any action would have probably exacerbated it!

Of course, I will admit that sometimes the endless memoranda from the sign-offs by desk officers and bureau chiefs prevent mistakes. I prepared a speech to be delivered in a conference in Rome. The talk announced a general reduction of economic aid. In my address I wanted to emphasize that the strength of a democratic republic is not merely defined by material tangibles, but by spiritual intangibles.

When the speech was approved, I was asked to give it a title. Over the phone I told my secretary, "Use the biblical phrase 'Man should not live on bread alone.'"

My secretary might not have heard me right. I got word back from Rome that the speech was delivered with the title: "Man Should Not Love in Bed Alone"!

My mission in the State Department was not to win the cold war but to persuade the cold world, or an indifferent America, to back the Nixon initiative for peace. Mike Collins, the astronaut, was an ideal spokesman. A Gary Cooper or Jimmy Stewart could best portray the hero's innate modesty and wholesome values. But such typecasting might shroud Collins's creativity.

Mike Collins was a poet, and you have only to read his book *Carrying the Flame* to realize it. For a speechwriter, it's no mean task to draft talks for a poet.

Yet, if Collins was poetic, he was also pragmatic. Commenting to me on Nixon's policy, he said, "The most successful idealist is the tough realist." It triggered a line I drafted for him: "We often see in the young idealists too many illusions, just as we may see in the old realists too few ideals."

Collins thought Nixon had vision in foreign policy. A former British prime minister and foreign secretary put it to me less kindly. In 1971, my wife and I were the guests of the Earl of Avon at his home near Salisbury. He is better remembered as Anthony Eden, who resigned after the Suez crisis. Eden had succeeded Churchill, and his wife, through a second marriage, was Churchill's niece, Clarissa.

In 1971, Lord Avon was the Conservative Party's leader in the House of Lords in the Heath government. Eden could not hide his disdain for John Foster Dulles, Eisenhower's secretary of state. He blamed Dulles for the U.S. opposition to the British–French operation to oust Nasser.

"Dulles," he said, "is too much the Calvinist. He reminded me of Gilbert and Sullivan's Bunthorne who was constantly uttering 'platitudes in stained-glass attitudes.' On the other hand," he continued, "Nixon—mind you, I only met him a couple of times and didn't much like him personally—but Nixon is a shrewd pragmatist who won't let pieties stand in the way of progress at the negotiation table."

Eden then told me about the time in 1952 when Prime Minister Churchill and Defense Minister Harold MacMillan flew to Cyprus to visit Archbishop Makarios, the leader of the emerging Cypriot nation.

Churchill asked MacMillan, "Harold, what kind of man is Makarios? Is he one of those ascetic, priestly men of the cloth concerned with spiritual rewards, or is he one of those nifty, scheming prelates interested in temporal gain?"

"Regrettably, Prime Minster," replied MacMillan, "the archbishop seems to be one of the latter."

"Good," said Churchill, clapping his hands. "Then he is one of my kind, and I can work with him."

The great leaders do possess vision, be it Churchill for Britain and the free world, de Gaulle for France, Chaim Weizman for Israel, or perhaps Makarios for Cyprus.

Eden told me that Churchill had more than vision. "Winston had not only the ability to see the future but the courage to recommend what should be done about it now.

"Churchill used to say to me, 'Anthony, there are two ways to prophesy the future; one is historically and the other scientifically. In the first, you look for patterns in the past that are applicable to the present. In the other, you take the data and statistics of today and project them ten or twenty years into the future.'"

In 1982, I was a Woodrow Wilson Fellow at the Center for International Scholars at the Smithsonian (I was researching my book *"My Fellow Americans": Presidential Addresses that Shaped History*) when retired Prime Minister Harold MacMillan joined us one night for dinner. The eighty-eight-year-old MacMillan, with all the languor of a former Etonian, told this story about Churchill.

"In early 1942, when frankly we were losing the war, I was resident minister for Algeria and I visited Churchill's headquarters in Casablanca. One evening he said to me, 'Harold, what kind of man do you think Cromwell was?'

"I didn't quite know what to say, so I offered, 'Very aggressive sort—don't you think, Prime Minister?'

"Churchill answered, 'Cromwell was obsessed with Spain but he never saw the danger of France.'

"The point was," MacMillan said to us, "that everyone was at the time concentrating on beating Hitler, but Churchill had already factored in the American involvement and Hitler's invasion of Russia and concluded that an allied victory would be inevitable—but that we should be addressing ourselves to the problem of the Soviet Union when the war was over."

In a day when so many politicians think "vision" is the answer to yesterday's newspaper headlines, vision such as Churchill's and Nixon's is a rare attribute.

I WAS ON MY WAY to an Omaha bookstore with my friend and former Nixon administration assistant attorney-general Wally Johnson when the car radio delivered the news on April 22 that former President Nixon had died. At the store, I was to autograph my latest book *The Wit and Wisdom of Winston Churchill*, foreword by Richard Nixon. The store event had been advertised by radio and newspaper. As a result, hundreds of Nebraskans queued up for me to autograph their book with the request that under my signature it would say, "April 22, 1994, Date of Death of President Richard Nixon."

I was also to go to Fort Worth to speak at a book luncheon, but I canceled it. Dianne and I flew out to the services at Yorba Linda. The night before the public ceremony, we drove in from our hotel next to the John Wayne (Orange County) Airport to pay our final respects. It was close to midnight, but the hard pelting rain did not deter a two-mile line of more than a thousand who felt compelled to do likewise.

With our special passes from Nixon Library Director John Taylor, we were ushered right into the viewing room. Before us were a black veteran and a construction worker. When the uniformed man doffed his hat and saluted, the worker took off his hard-hat helmet and saluted, too. Two of the Silent Majority had offered their final respects.

At the services the next afternoon, I sat in a row with Bill Safire and Ray Price. Even before the ceremonies commenced and the four presidents—Ford, Reagan, Bush, and Clinton—took their seats, the music "You'll Never Walk Alone" made my eyes tear up.

Before the ceremonies, I saw my friend Jonathan Aitken who, along with former Prime Minister Edward Heath, was representing Great Britain. He told me of seeing Nixon only a few weeks before when Nixon was coming back from Moscow. He said that at Heathrow, Nixon called, "Jonathan, would you like to see a show?" Nixon refused the limousine that cabinet member Aitken offered, but met him at the theater. The show was *Carousel*. At intermission, a group of fifty U.S. servicemen from Germany on a weekend pass recognized the former president and stood. The rest of the London audience joined the cheers.

Aitken noted that during the song, "You'll Never Walk Alone," he could see Nixon weeping.

Afterward, as they walked along the Strand by the Thames together, Nixon said, "I guess you think I was pretty mushy." He then told Aitken that it was Pat's favorite song. They had seen *Carousel* together in New York when Nixon returned from World War II. "I played it for Pat on the piano, Jonathan, just before I took her to the hospital that final time."

Nixon accepted Jonathan's invitation to his London flat that evening to deliver another one of his *tour d'horizon* foreign policy addresses to a group of British parliamentarians and academics. As was his custom, Nixon never consulted notes as he addressed the living room audience for an hour and a half, replete with conversations he had with various world leaders. At the end, Aitken said, "Mr. President, you'll come back next year and do another?"

"No," said Nixon, "this was my last. This is goodbye, Jonathan."

Chapter Thirteen

FORD WRITER

He was wont to speak plain and to the purpose like an honest man.
MUCH ADO ABOUT NOTHING

was not living in Washington when President Nixon resigned. I watched it on television with Don Whitehead in my Chestnut Hill house.

I had returned to Philadelphia in 1972, snagging some corporate clients (mostly for lobbying) on the basis of what I quoted Alice Roosevelt Longworth as saying, "the illusion of access to power."

Like a desert mirage, the illusion soon disappeared in the miasma of the Watergate morass.

Any moves to dig up new clients were stymied. I was like a Hester Prynne in the *Scarlet Letter*, not wearing an "A," but a big red "N" for Nixon. Those years in the service of Nixon had to be just about eliminated in any resume.

So, when a call came to write speeches for Ford, I jumped at the chance. Better to be typed as a speechwriter for presidents than as a Nixon speechwriter. Actually, though I worked in the White House, I received my checks from Jim Baker, who was heading up the reelection effort.

In a talk to a British audience, I once used Churchill's description of Russia to describe Nixon: "He is a riddle, wrapped in a mystery, inside an enigma."

Well, if you strip down Gerry Ford, every layer would be a nice guy. He is decency, wrapped in geniality, inside banality. Ford was neither insecure nor neurotically intense. Why should he be? As a young man he had the looks of a male model and the physique to make the All-American second team as center for the Michigan Wolverines.

Reporters loved to make fun of Ford's clumsiness. Just because a man over six feet tall bumps into airplane ceilings does not mean he's clumsy. Yes, he did slip on an icy step from an airplane and like most golfers he often slices, but few of those newsmen in their thirties could match a seventy- or even eighty-year-old Ford's grace and prowess on the golf course or ski slopes.

Everyone recalls LBJ's bon mot: "Gerry Ford couldn't think and chew gum at the same time." It is instructive to note that Ford, at Yale Law School, graduated with higher standing than fellow classmates Cyrus Vance and Sargeant Shriver, who served under LBJ as well as JFK.

If he lacked the quick wit of Jack Kennedy, he had the staying power that often wins the higher grades. For one thing, he had the kind of head that could absorb statistics. When I was out in Vail with him in the summer of 1977, I was astonished at his mastery of missile payloads and budget intricacies. He was a walking encyclopedia of every budget for the past fifteen years.

Yet, as a deliverer of speeches he was pedestrian. He was comfortable with the kind of stock speeches given to the Grand Rapids Chamber of Commerce but little else. In speechwriting, Nixon edited you heavily in substance, Reagan edited you in style, but Ford didn't edit you at all. The first time I drafted a talk for him, he sent back a memo of praise. But when I found out he did it for everyone, the compliment deflated like a fallen soufflé.

From the writer's point of view, Ford had the annoying habit of inserting ad-lib remarks in a slangy style that clashed with the rhythm of the prepared text.

One time in 1976, he crossed from the White House to the Renwick House to speak at a reception honoring Pat Moynihan, who was resigning from the United Nations to run for the Senate in New York.

In the remarks, I had Ford praise Moynihan's outspoken warnings to the third world nations: "Ambassador Moynihan brought a strong measure of realism to newly independent states of Africa. He told them they had freed themselves from the shackles of European colonialism only to assume new chains of military Marxism." Then Ford ad-libbed, "What I'm really trying to say is that Pat Moynihan really called a spade a spade."

Ford secured his nomination in Kansas City by putting his incumbency against the idealism of movement conservatives. For the fall campaign, Ford was like an old war horse confined to the stable when he heard the bugles of a cavalry charge. Yet, interestingly, the polls showed that Ford dipped in the polls every time he left the White House for the hustings. On the other hand, the evening's news each day that highlighted a presidential appearance in the Rose Garden meeting with foreign leaders or announcing a presidential program steadily narrowed the gap between him and Governor Jimmy Carter.

I did come up with one campaign ploy I called "adjectival assassination," or what ad writers call subliminal transference. If there was one adjective to describe Carter that even partisan Democrats would agree to, it was "strange." The *Playboy* interview ("lust in my heart"), the sighting of UFOs, his slighting references to the immorality of LBJ, and even his born-again evangelism all reinforced the uneasy feeling, even among liberals, about Carter as compared to "old shoe" Gerry Ford.

We fed these announcements to the White House press: "We find very *odd* Governor Carter's remarks about Korea." "It strikes us as *strange* that Governor Carter would select as foreign policy adviser…"

I searched my *Roget's* and came up with "bizarre," "weird," "eccentric," "peculiar"—all to reinforce the queasy feelings Democrats might have about the Democratic candidate.

In 1996, the Clinton campaign adopted the same ploy on Bob Dole. "Old," "tired," and even "grumpy" were used to describe comments or programs by the senator.

My one regret, however, in Ford's campaign was the closing remarks that the president forgot to use at the end of his crucial October televised debate:

> I became president in one of the most difficult periods in our nation's history. I tried to do my level best. I don't say that I completely succeeded, but I think you will agree that times seem brighter than they were then. All of you remember the tall ships and wagon trains of last July Fourth. Millions of people from New York to San Francisco, without a riot or single incident, celebrated their heritage. They rang bells, sang in churches, and danced in the streets. More than any mission to the Moon or Mars, this spontaneous outpouring of affection proved to the world that America has regained her role as the guardian of democratic hopes and dreams.
>
> I don't claim to have done this. You, the American people, by reaching back into your own roots, rekindled our pride. No president by signing a paper or enacting a bill can lift the spirit of the nation. He can only hope by setting the right tone and charting a true course that he helped restore the faith and renew confidence.
>
> This I tried to do. I tried to heal the wounds of War and Watergate. I tried to check inflation and revive a depressed economy. I know I haven't completely

succeeded—I know I've made my share of mistakes—
but I ask you to let me finish the job.

For the finale, I flipped through my files of "soul-shakers"—
poignant, emotional anecdotes to inspire audiences—for one about
Ike—Ford's particular hero whose rugged, solid, good looks, and
genial good will he seemed to evoke.

> Years ago, just about the time I came to Congress, my
> good friend General Eisenhower bought a farm in
> Gettysburg. At the recording of the deed in the court-
> house, a clerk asked him "General, why, when you live
> in New York and have a house provided for you as
> president of Columbia University, do you want this land
> in Pennsylvania?"
> And General Eisenhower replied, "I want one time in
> my life to take a piece of earth and return it to God
> better than I found it."
> With God's help, will you join me in making our
> land a brighter land for our children and our children's
> children?

Perhaps the reason Ford failed to use my closer was his bonehead
answer to the question on Poland.

Ford's answer that Poland was still "free" came about because he
didn't remember to do what teachers always warn their students
against: don't jump to answer until you have considered the question
carefully.

In the sample questions fed to the president in preparation for the
debate, there was one about the Solidarity movement in which he
would talk about the "free" spirit of the Polish people. When Ford
heard "Poland," it triggered his canned answer to the Polish people
question.

Ford's best issue in the 1976 campaign was foreign policy, but he blew it with that answer. The gap between him and Carter, which had been steadily closing, suddenly began to widen for Carter. (The Ford campaign would not build momentum until the closing week, and by then it was too late.)

Our advice to Ford before the debate was one word: peace. His handlers told him to wedge into every answer, regardless of the question, this statement: "Let me say again that I take pride that no American boys are dying for the first time in over a decade and that we have *peace*."

But it was "Poland," not "Peace," that was remembered after the Philadelphia debate. The constant media replay of Ford's answer did not help.

When the media find a sore, they pick it open and then zoom in with the camera to show the blood. If it heals, they break the scab and repeat the close-up examination. The first polls by viewers, right after the debate, had Ford winning, but after the TV replays the "dumbness" of Ford took over.

It is sad that Ford should be remembered for this gaffe, since a guiding tenet of his career was a resolute commitment to defend Europe against Communism. When he came to Washington in 1949, the Republican Party was still shaking off its isolationist past. From his very first term, Republican Ford supported the Democrat President Truman in his policies on NATO, the Marshall Plan, and the Point Four Doctrine.

Because of that, I urged Ford in 1978, after he left office, to make what is sometimes called at Westminster College "the second Iron Curtain address." I was in Vail helping Ford with his memoirs when I looked through his speech invitations, among them a letter from Westminster College inviting him to speak on March 4, 1978, on the thirty-second anniversary of the Iron Curtain address. (The next year, I would be the thirty-third annual speaker.)

I had also just submitted to my publisher my biography, *Churchill:*

Speaker of the Century. As a result, I had developed some expertise on that speech and its background.

I suggested to Ford that we use the Fulton forum to speak out against Carter's silence about the upcoming elections in France and Italy where the Communist Parties in both countries were leading in the polls. Every president, Democrat or Republican, since Harry Truman had publicly spelled out the dangers to the countries in Western Europe of a Communist Party government.

Ford opened his speech:

> Thirty-two years ago a leader of one of the great Western democracies—defeated and out of office— came to this college to warn the world against Communism. In no way could I compare myself to the one who made the phrase "Iron Curtain" part of the Cold War language, yet I yield to no one—including Churchill—in my love of freedom and my hatred of tyranny.

In the address, Ford attacked Carter for his failure as the leader of the free world to speak out about the danger of voting Communist. He pointed out that in Czechoslovakia, Poland, and Hungary, the Communist Party won a plurality as a minority party in a multiparty system and then engineered a one-party system.

And to those who argued that the French and Italian Communist Parties were not puppets pulled by Kremlin strings, Ford reminded them that in the recent Communist Party Congresses in France and Italy, they had endorsed recent Soviet aggressions in Afghanistan by unanimous vote. Unanimous votes on key questions, said Ford, occur only in totalitarian states.

He also predicted that if France and Italy voted in Communist governments, it would more than likely nudge Spain and Portugal to follow suit.

Ford closed:

> During the power shortage a couple of years ago, the Capitol dome was turned off even when Congress was in session. It saddened me when I drove away from a darkened Capitol, because I always somehow imagined the dome was lit by the friction of free debate and the fiery clash of ideas.
>
> Lord Grey, the British foreign secretary, said in 1914, just before World War I, "I see the lights going out in Europe."
>
> And I see the lights of liberty in parliaments in Paris, Rome, and even Madrid and Lisbon being snuffed out unless the free world leaders voice what a Winston Churchill would say if he were here today.

I took more pride in that speech than any other I have ever written because it may have changed history. Zbigniew Brzezinski told me later that President Carter, at his urging, lifted his silence and went to France to deliver his warning. After Carter's talk, support for the Communists tumbled in both France and Italy and they lost in the elections. Both *Le Monde* in Paris and the Vatican's *Osservatore* endorsed Ford's speech and demanded that President Carter speak out. Brezinski said that one reason Carter changed his mind about "not interfering with European elections" was his fear that if the map of Western Europe were painted red from Italy to Portugal by 1980, he would be defeated for reelection if Ford reminded the nation of his warning.

I had gone to Vail in the summer of 1977, as I said, to be an editorial adviser for Ford's memoirs. My good friend, Trevor Armbrister, set it up. Trevor, a senior editor at *Reader's Digest,* is a true professional who doesn't let adjectives clutter his attention to facts and details.

I was brought in, as Ford later said, "to put the raisins in the muffin." Or to put it another way, I was the "color man" in a play-by-play broadcast. But extracting anecdotes from the prosaic Ford was a daunting task.

At the end of the day, Trevor and I would join the former president in the Bass Lodge for a drink. That was to be my best shot for hearing some unguarded reminiscences. Ford would drink martinis from a tall tumbler. Two or even three would not dent his genial stolidity. I would try to match him martini for martini in my quest for anecdotes. Then I would rush back to my quarters to put down some notes before the martinis overtook my memory.

I did contribute in fashioning some of his personal credos and beliefs. Ford reacted enthusiastically to my having him include Sir Kenneth Clark's closing valedictory in his Civilization lecture, which he had heard when he came to Washington in 1970.

> I reveal myself in my true colors as a stick-in-the-mud.
> I believe that order is better than chaos, creation better
> than destruction. I prefer gentleness to violence, forgive-
> ness to vendetta... Above all, I believe in the God-given
> genius of certain individuals, and I value a society that
> makes their existence possible.

Yet, I was not able to elicit any philosophical musings on the presidency as an institution. Unlike Nixon who seized the opportunity to challenge the historian or political scientist who knew about government only in abstract theory, Ford was bored by talk of political philosophy or history. Our conversations had all the bland conviviality of a Saturday night dinner at the country club—with one difference.

Ford was not a gossiper. Presidents, like most politicians, would put a village yenta to shame. Ford did not relish the morsels of personal peccadillos.

Ford would shrug off mention of a friend's apostasy or a beneficiary's ingratitude. An LBJ, JFK or Nixon might explode in unexpurgated Anglo-Saxon at the mention of such disloyalty—not Ford.

The only two people that triggered any vehement reaction were John Dean and James Schlessinger—Dean for his ass-kissing amorality and Schlessinger for his self-proclaimed monopoly of superior wisdom. (He once lectured Ford at a cabinet meeting on how to deal with Speaker Tip O'Neill, whom Ford had known for close to three decades.)

In trivia games, I win barroom bets with historical buffs on this curiosity: "What President was also a King?" (Some have mentioned various presidents as also being king of Hawaii!) The answer is Ford. He was born Leslie King. He took the name of his stepfather, Gerald Ford, who adopted him after his biological father left his mother.

When Ford was asked about the time he first met his biological father, he paused and delivered his answer without emotional inflection. Ford had been at a drugstore when his father introduced himself: "Hello, Gerry. I'm your dad." He would not comment on any emotional trauma. He had put it behind him.

Decency and straight-forwardness define Ford, but sometimes he let it work to his disadvantage. On one occasion in Vail, Ford set off for a round of golf. I accompanied him. Ahead was a golfer whose play seemed to be almost in slow motion.

I asked if he would let former President Ford play through since he had a TV interview at 4:00 P.M. The duffer replied, "Just because a guy's been president of the United States doesn't mean... " I left and went back to report to Ford.

Much later when Ford had completed his eighteenth hole and was striding smartly to make his TV interview, who comes strutting up to ask Ford to autograph some golf cards but the same snail-paced golfer. The great thing about Ford is that he stopped to sign his cards. The bad thing is that he did. He should have said, "I would, but I don't have time now."

On the way to the Bass Lodge, Ford said, "Jamie, I know that one question on the TV show will be about the announcement by President Carter that he has cut the White House Staff by 20 percent. You and I know that he hasn't actually cut it but that the payroll of those staffers is now being picked up by the Interior or HUD. You always have a good anecdote…"

"Well, Mr. President," I said, "in 1929 the newly elected President Hoover announced that he was eliminating the riding horses at the White House. When former President Coolidge was asked about it at his home in Plymouth, Vermont, he replied laconically, 'So where are the horses feeding now, Ft. Myers?' In other words, no horses were killed—it was just that some other part of the government was feeding them."

When Robert Pierpoint of CBS posed the White House personnel question to Ford, he answered, "Well, Jamie Humes tells this great story about Hoover and Coolidge…"

Again, Ford was kind enough to mention my name, but because he did the story wasn't used in the taped interview. I can assure you that a Kennedy, Nixon, or Reagan would have run with the anecdote without my name.

A sense of humanity or compassion is not what impelled Ford to pardon Nixon. It was a decision made by his head—not his heart—for he knew at the time that it might cost him reelection in 1976.

As a lawyer, he believed in the rule of law and no one—not even the president—was above the law. But law school also teaches you that in rare instances, necessity, for reasons of public policy, might override legal precedent.

Ford had watched the appeal of Bob Haldeman string out over three years. Nixon, who had available to him the constitutional protections of his office, could extend the court process for years more. Not only that, but Nixon could reveal some CIA secrets about both Presidents Kennedy and Johnson, who gave tacit approval to assassinations, attempted coups d'état, and were involved in other dubious intrigues.

"The appeal process will go past 1976, and in the meantime," Ford told me, "I would not be able to get the nation's attention on any issue—the headlines would be all Watergate and the Nixon case. It was time to turn the page and begin anew."

Ford began the healing process, and that was the title I suggested to him for his memoirs. He was leaning toward *Straight from the Shoulder*. I suggested *A Time to Heal*, which comes right from a passage in Ecclesiastics.

> A time to sow and a time to reap.
> A time to mourn and a time to rejoice.
> A time to kill and *a time to heal*.

Ford told me, "Jamie, you know when I was elected in 1948, one of the big issues was Nixon and the Hiss case, and when I was defeated one of the big issues was the pardon of Nixon."

If Ford had not pardoned Nixon, he would not have healed the nation. On the other hand, he might have rewon the presidency. In the 1976 campaign, Carter employed the Cicero gambit to raise the pardon issue. Rhetoricians give it the term "praeterito." I call it the "clean-sounding dirty politician ploy."

Carter would purposely say, "I will not raise the issue of Ford's pardon of President Nixon, and I have asked all my staff not to talk about the pardon." And in doing so, he of course brought it up. Cicero started it in his Roman Senate debate about Cataline: "I will pass over the scandal..."

When Senator Kennedy ran against Carter for the 1980 Democratic nomination, the president would say, "I have asked that Chappaquiddick not be mentioned." In the 1952 presidential campaign Nixon wielded it against Adlai Stevenson: "I will not talk about Governor Stevenson's divorce. His divorce is not an issue..."

On the lecture circuit, in my "Confessions of a White House Ghost" (this book takes the title from the talk), I often quote this

Churchill nugget to describe Carter: "History tells us never to trust any man who has not a single redeeming vice."

In Atlanta after my speech, one woman raised this question:

"Mr. Humes, that's not quite true about vices—why, President Carter said he had 'lust in his heart.'"

"Madam," I replied, "I barely passed biology in Williams College, but one thing I did learn is that the heart is not the organ in which lust resides."

I met Carter only once, and that was before he ran for president. As a consultant for Don Whitehead's Appalachian Regional Commission, I was with him when he briefed Governor Carter on a proposed Nixon program. Carter believed that the program would help Alabama and North Carolina, to the detriment of Georgia. And he said to us, "I'm going to get down on my knees and pray that the Lord in his infinite wisdom opens the eyes of the administration to see the injustice perpetrated on the people of Georgia."

I didn't mind Carter opposing the program, but to invoke the Lord's name was a bit much. I kept myself from answering, "Well, Governor, I just came down from the mountain, and my back aches from carrying those slabs of stone, and this is what I've been commanded to say…"

Carter deserves credit for his peace efforts in bringing Anwar Sadat and Menachem Begin together. But it makes me wonder, if both Carter and Begin claimed direct lines to God, which would be the Holy Writ?

Carter is not my favorite president, but I have to say that I took a liking to his sister, the evangelist Ruth Carter Stapleton. I was promoting a book of mine at the Boston Book Fair at the Copley Plaza in September 1976, and the managers of the fair thought it would be a good idea to stage a debate of the Democratic candidate's sister and a member of the Ford White House staff. "No way," I answered. I was not going to be put in the position of attacking the presidential candidate's sister. I could see the headlines "Ford Aide Attacks Carter's Sister."

We did, however, meet in a hotel suite. She was living proof that an evangelist can be brimming with fun and personality.

At one point she said, "You know the difference between my brother Jimmy and Billy... Well, I had this problem, so I went to Jimmy and told him about it. He said, 'Ruth Ellen,' as he took my hand, 'let us pray together for God's help.'

"Now Billy, when I told him the problem I had, he went out, got a can of beer and his checkbook, then after a couple of swallows he pulled out a pen and said, 'Ruth Ellen, put in what you need. If I don't have enough I'll get a loan.'"

Yet, for a teetotaling, Sunday-school-teaching Baptist, Carter did inspire loyalty from his good ol' boy aides like Hamilton Jordan and Jody Powell. Sometimes it bordered on the excessive. In early 1980, when my biography of Churchill had just come out, I went to the White House with my Democratic friend, J.D. Williams. There we met Carter's head of Congressional Liaison, who hailed from Macon, Georgia.

When J.D. showed my book to the aide, he said approvingly, "Winston Churchill. I guess he's just about the only other man in the twentieth century who can rank up there with Jimmy Carter." I thought blasphemy was a cardinal sin, even for Baptists!

At that point, I wished I could have unscrewed one of those Jack Daniels miniatures I'd left in some White House desks on the last day of the Ford White House in January 1977. All Ford staff had received notes to turn in their White House passes before noon on Inauguration Day. I was resolved to wait until the very last minute. I even engaged a photographer to take a shot of the White House policeman ripping off my pinned badge at 11:59 A.M.

Just before stepping out the West Gate exit to surrender my badge, I went through the empty offices in the West Wing. Rooms with desks containing only phones, and walls displaying only hooks are depressing until you tell yourself that a transition is proof of democracy. To sustain the weary aides of a teetotaling president, I put the

Jack Daniels back in the Oval Office desk drawer. I also left the typed verses of Robert Frost's "Snowy Woods" to remind the president of the expansive pledges he had made in the campaign.

> And I have promises to keep
> And miles to go before I sleep.

Chapter Fourteen

THE GREAT COMMUNICATOR

When he speaks, the air a chartered libertine is still.
HENRY V

T he first speech I ever wrote for Ronald Reagan wound up in the Guinness book of bloopers. It was 1975. Reagan had left the governor's office in Sacramento and was gearing up for a 1976 presidential campaign against Ford. When Reagan received an invitation to speak to the World Affairs Council of Philadelphia, his staff saw it as an opportunity to burnish his foreign policy credentials. Researchers at a Georgetown University think tank had drafted a talk outlining a policy position on Asia and Africa. I was to smooth out the academic language into rhetoric. The phrase "third world" occurred seven times.

Since I was then serving on the board of the World Affairs Council, I attended the luncheon at the Bellevue Stratford Hotel in Philadelphia. At my table was our former ambassador to Britain, Walter Annenberg, and Pennsylvania Senator Dick Schweiker. When someone asked me if I had any role in the address by Reagan, I modestly demurred in such a way to imply a possible involvement.

Midway through the first page of the speech, which I had pulled out of my pocket to follow, Reagan said, "We must address the needs of a Third World *War*." He did this six more times.

The press gleefully brandished it as a Freudian slip that revealed his troglodyte views. It also confirmed the Beltway wisdom that he was a second-rate actor who couldn't follow his lines.

As one who viewed his performance both in his *King's Row* movie and the 1966 TV debate with Senator Robert Kennedy, I agreed with Nixon, who said, "The political landscape is littered with those who underestimated Ronald Reagan." Still, in 1979, I chose to work for George Bush instead of Reagan. (One reason was that George Bush called me.)

Reagan was an actor. In fact, he told Walter Cronkite in an interview in 1984 that he couldn't imagine being a president without an actor's talents. Franklin Roosevelt, Reagan's hero for emulation, is a prize exhibit of that belief.

Yet, film star experience does not in itself make an actor a great speaker, as George Murphy and Shirley Temple Black attest. (I once tried, without success, to write a lecture tour talk for Cary Grant. He was terrified of speaking. So, I wrote a series of answers to questions that women might ask him. "What is your definition of taste?" "Who was your favorite heroine?")

Usually, the only actors who can deliver convincing speeches are Shakespeareans who are used to orations such as Mark Anthony's eulogy in *Julius Caesar* or King Henry's battle speech at Agincourt in *Henry V*.

Reagan became a skilled communicator through his experience as a spokesman for General Electric. He had to address employees and business groups, sometimes three times a day, four times a week. And, of course, the speech that launched his political career was his nationally televised appeal for Senator Goldwater in October 1964. "A Time for Choosing" was the culmination of polishing and repolishing his five-by-eight notecards.

Those notecards had lines written out in a kind of shorthand: Amer., govt, dem, rts (America, government, democracy, rights) with verbs and prepositions often omitted. Govt big eno give-big eno take. (A government big enough to give you what you want is big enough to take it away.) He also was his own speech coach. In his drafts you can see stress marks before certain words (/ or // or ///). They indicated the length of pause for emphasis. The delivery may have seemed natural but he had the experience of hundreds of rehearsals. He had market-tested the product.

William Jennings Bryan's oration "The Cross of Gold" was tried out in hundreds of earlier renditions before grange and farm groups. The same refining process was used by Dr. Martin Luther King for his "I Have a Dream" speech in 1967 by appearing before scores of churches and civil rights groups. Only by repetition do the phrases become second nature, and then the speaker learns to master the pause and the change of modulation that are the hallmarks of a stirring and persuasive speaker.

Think for a moment of the stories you've told a hundred times— the first time you met your spouse or that first hole-in-one. You don't have to refer to notes or script. You have it down so pat that you can concentrate on your listeners. You have come to know just when to pause for effect or lower your voice.

That's why Reagan used so many anecdotes. Every other page in a text for a Reagan address would be "the pony story" or "a city on the hill."

On the latter, I like to think I had an input. In 1974, Chuck Manatt hosted a Beverly Hills party for my book *Instant Eloquence*. The final section is devoted to "Soul-Shakers"—closers to inspire audiences. One of them is John Winthrop's "We must always consider that we shall be as a city upon a hill—the eyes of all people upon us." By the way, that was how Reagan concluded his talk to his supporters when he lost to Ford in Kansas City in 1976.

The best of stories Reagan would never use on television. As he said to me, "Jamie, once I tell it to a national audience, I can never use it again."

But Reagan also mastered the art of reading a text between the anecdotes. It always amazes me how so many politicians, preachers, or public personalities, except for TV types, settle into a wooden trance of delivery.

As a communications consultant, I teach "the Reagan method": NEVER LET WORDS COME OUT OF YOUR MOUTH WHILE YOU ARE LOOKING DOWN AT NOTES OR TEXT. Reagan learned this, not as an actor, but as a radio communicator in Iowa. He was fired from his first radio job because he could not read the commercials convincingly. When the man who replaced him moved on, "Dutch" Reagan asked for a second chance. In the meantime, Reagan had worked out how to make radio ads sound conversational. He would look down at a line of the ad, then cover it up with his hand and conversationalize what he had photographed with his eye. The pauses, when he was looking down, not only made the words more readily grasped but approximated the natural flow of conversation.

As a frequent speaker, I learned another trick from Reagan. I eat next to nothing before a talk, sipping only hot water. Before an address, Reagan underwent this ritual: he had hot water on hand, not even tea, and a chocolate chip cookie, usually wrapped in aluminum foil.

"The cookie's for energy," Reagan would explain. "The hot water, I learned from an old preacher and a singer friend of mine—you see, ice water constricts the vocal chords."

It turned out that the preacher and the singer were Billy Graham and Frank Sinatra!

Reagan slips in two contact lenses when reading addresses—the left, far-sighted one for looking at the audience, and the right, near-sighted one for reading the script.

But don't think that Reagan was just a performer who knew how to read a script. He often had better ideas than the speechwriter. He would recast the words to fit his own easy conversational style. As two people who once wrote speeches for him, Martin Anderson and John McClaughry, told me, Reagan's best speechwriter was himself.

If a Sorensen had written for Reagan, "Ask not what your country can do for you..." he would have rewritten it. Reagan would sacrifice quotability for credibility.

Such jeweled rhetoric would sound pretentious if said over the back fence to a neighbor or to a guy on the next bar stool. Reagan's own criterion was, "Would you talk that way to your barber?" (He had a barber in Santa Barbara whom he always imagined he was addressing.)

When a wordsmith thinks he has crafted a timeless line, he often sets it up with the "magic marker" gimmick—"So my fellow citizens..." or "Let me say to you..." Sam Rosenman wrote for Franklin Roosevelt in his Inaugural Address of 1935, "*Let me again repeat my firm belief that the only thing* we have to fear is fear itself." Are we to assume that FDR in the rest of the speech was less than sincere? Sorensen telegraphed his memorial line, "*And so my fellow countrymen*, ask not what the country can do for you..." Well, who was JFK speaking to in an Inaugural Address? Germans? Frenchmen?

Reagan believed that such rhetorical tricks could make you sound like a state senator windbag at a country fair. ("And I say to you, my fellow citizens...")

In my speech course at the University of Pennsylvania, I give my students an acronym for crafting memorable lines. C-R-E-A-M— contrast, rhyme, echo, alliteration, and metaphor. "Echo" refers to the repetition of a word or phrase, such as the celebrated lines in the Roosevelt and Kennedy inaugurals.

Kennedy's quotable with the echo ring is "Let us never fear to negotiate but let us never negotiate out of fear." A couple of days before the Reagan 1981 inaugural, Tony Dolan, his writer, while having a drink with me at the Hay-Adams, showed me his echo contribution: "So I say to you, if we love our country, why don't we also love our countrymen?" Reagan, however, would cut the prefatory "magic marker" and rewrite it to say, "How can we love our country and not love our countrymen?"

If Reagan had left the Dolan line unchanged, it might have ended up in *Bartlett's Quotations* the way so many of Roosevelt's and Kennedy's utterances have. After all, many sentences from presidential Inaugural Addresses do. Reagan was called the "Great Communicator" but few of his exact words, except for "evil empire," are quoted. He connected with the "man in the street" by displaying his heart and his humor. Reagan knew more about what made speeches work than did his speechwriters. He should have. He had delivered a thousand of them. To Reagan, statistics were for bureaucrats and quotations for the pedantic.

Sorensen amassed for Kennedy reams of quotations from Aristotle to Zola. Kennedy quoted from the likes of T.S. Eliot, Edward Gibbon, Tolstoy, Cervantes, Aeschylus, and Rousseau—to name a few. Unlike Kennedy, Reagan wouldn't quote a line from Eliot's *The Wasteland* to his barber and so he wouldn't to the American people.

Reagan had his own files, and they included a lot of quotations, but most of the quotations he collected were embedded in anecdotes.

Reagan liked to tell and hear good stories—not just those that were funny but those that struck a patriotic chord or illustrated a point about government waste or the human spirit. I told him once about meeting the retired rector at an Anglican Church near Chartwell. He once chided Churchill for his irregular attendance, and the old statesman replied, "I am not a pillar of the church but a buttress—supporting it from the outside."

But Churchill knew his Bible, and I recounted to Reagan's nodding assent how Churchill told friends that Jesus never used the word "salvation" in his sermons.

I said, "Governor, that was Greek theological abstraction. Instead, Churchill would tell how Jesus would relate the story of how the prodigal son who wasted his money on wine and women and then came back to say, "Dad, give me a second chance.'"

Reagan said abstract words go in one ear and out the other but a good story paints an unforgettable picture.

Reagan was a good listener and would glean from conversations the potential of a possible anecdote or story.

He heard one from Marine General Kelley, which he turned into a "wet eye" closer when he addressed the nation on the terrorist attack in Lebanon.

> One of the Marines who was injured in that terrorist attack on our compound in Beirut was completely burned. There he lay on the hospital bed, swathed in bandages from head to foot.
>
> One day, Marine Commandant P.C. Kelley visited the hospital and approached the boy's bed. When Kelley introduced himself, the boy couldn't believe it was actually the commandant. Since he couldn't see, he reached out to touch the four stars on his shoulder.
>
> Then the Marine motioned with his two hands for a pencil and paper. It was brought in, and he scratched out on the pad "Semper Fi."

"Semper Fideles—Always Faithful," Reagan repeated. "And don't you think we should keep faith with our boys?"

The Reagan White House did request one quotation from me. It was Reagan's first state dinner, and he held it for his favorite leader and special friend, Prime Minister Margaret Thatcher.

Reagan knew that Churchill was Thatcher's hero, and I was called to dig up some Churchill quotes for his banquet toast.

Because Thatcher relished the clash of political combat, I forwarded Churchill's line when he escaped an ambush in 1897. "There is nothing more exhilarating than to be shot at without result."

In the cursory newspaper coverage of the dinner, the words by Churchill in the toast to Thatcher were not mentioned. Months later, they would echo around the world. When Reagan was shot at the Washington Hilton, he was rushed to George Washington University Hospital. There, stripped for surgery, lying on the gurney, Reagan uttered, "You know what Churchill said, 'There's nothing more exhilarating than to be shot at without result.'"

I sent another quotation to the White House at the time of the *Challenger* space launch disaster. I remembered that in the church across from the White House next to LaFayette Square (St. John's Episcopal), the rector, John Magee, in a sermon, read a letter his son, John, Jr., a Royal Canadian Air Force pilot, had written just before being shot down.

> And while with silent lifting grace I've trod
> The high untrespassed sanctity of space
> Put out my hand and touched the face of God.

Churchill once wrote of a politician in the 1930s who "looked at a leaf with a microscopic eye but never scaled the mountain to view the forest." That wasn't true of Reagan! Carter might have read every piece of legislation as he claimed, but if so, it was a waste of his valuable presidential time. I ask you, how many of you actually read every word of your own insurance policy? Reagan didn't involve himself in the legislative process. He was the chief executive.

Actually, the Founding Fathers intended that the president be "an elected King," and George Washington created the role that shaped the institution of the presidency.

Both Roosevelts, as well as Eisenhower and Kennedy, instinctively understood that part of being president is being "king." They didn't carry their own bags, like Carter, and tell what kind of underwear they wore, like Clinton. Actor Reagan performed the role with easy grace and aplomb.

But away from the public eye, Reagan was more distant than his warm image suggested. Though always genial and in good humor, few politicians were his intimates. Speechwriters were never sure he even knew their names.

During the 1980 campaign, I was the president of Kingstree Communications, a speech-counseling operation. Its chairman was Lee Bowman, Jr., who in 1979 had succeeded his father of the same name and who had been an actor and a friend of Reagan.

Lee asked me if I could get him in to see Governor Reagan when he was speaking in New York. I was doubtful but I dutifully relayed the request. To my surprise, Reagan saw him for an hour. His staff had to drag him away from talking to Lee. Afterward, I asked Lee, "What did he say about the campaign?" "Campaign? We talked Hollywood."

Politics bored Reagan but not political principles. A former Democrat, he had the conviction of the converted. In his continual preparation for his talks as spokesman for General Electric, the collection of newspaper items and writing out of lines on those old five-by-eight cards speeded the switch from a Roosevelt Democrat to a Goldwater Republican.

As a movement conservative, Reagan held certain core beliefs about communism, freedom, and the limitation of freedom. No adviser could dissuade him to depart from those principles.

At the Reykjavik summit, Premier Gorbachev insisted that the Soviets would not make any concessions on strategic arms cuts unless we gave up the SDI (Strategic Defense Initiative). The U.S. diplomats wrung their hands when Reagan overrode Secretary of State George Shultz's advice and said, "The meeting is over. We're leaving!"

An adamant Reagan flew home without a joint statement or any signatures.

Tony Dolan told me that Reagan's advisers, including Jim Baker, tried to no avail to talk Reagan out of his "Marxism on the Ash-heap of History" address to the British Houses of Parliament (where he predicted the imminent collapse of the Soviet Union).

Jim Reichley, the former Brookings Institution scholar in residence on Republicanism and conservatism, told me a salient difference between the Reagan and Bush White House operations. In the Reagan White House, some top aide, when discussing a certain policy position, would say, "Well, this issue has not yet come to the president's attention, but knowing his principles and beliefs it is safe to say he will support [or oppose] X."

But, said Reichley, under President Bush, a Dick Darman or John Sunnunu would "announce" a Bush stand; however one was sure whether it reflected Bush's thinking—because Bush had no defined credo.

Pat Robertson, speaking about Bush, told me in 1986: "George is a Christian, a patriot, and a gentleman, and that about covers the extent of his beliefs."

That's not the worst thing you can say about someone. Bush's sterling character, along with his experience, is part of the reason I backed Bush in 1979 against Reagan. Like so many eastern Republicans, as well as Democrats, I underestimated his leadership qualities (I also thought Bush would run better against Carter).

In addition, like so many others in the Republican Party, I was cultivated by Bush. It has been said that George Bush signed more notes than Chase Manhattan. At the retail level he far exceeded Reagan or any other Republican candidate in history.

He recognized the names and faces of more Californians than Reagan and possibly more Kansans than Dole. He probably knows more people by name than any politician in history, including the legendary Jim Farley (FDR's postmaster-general).

The difference between Reagan and Bush is their card files. Reagan compiled five-by-eight cards for speeches, but Bush had three-by-five cards on people. Bush's singular success as president, his "Desert Storm" victory, owes much to his retail technique. A

Margaret Thatcher or a Nixon would have intervened in August 1990 without Senate authorization. Bush opted for the hard way, lining up UN endorsement first to mount pressure and support for Senate approval (even then he carried the Senate Resolution by only two votes).

As a former UN ambassador envoy to China, CIA chief, and vice president for eight years, Bush put the contacts and acquaintances he had cultivated for years to good use. He could call a head of government and say, "Hello, Mohammed, how's your wife, Fatima?" The presidents and prime ministers warmed to these personal overtures. (Of course, by agreeing to a UN umbrella, he would be constrained from marching on to Baghdad.)

But, on the whole, in today's mass communications, Reagan's mastery of wholesale marketing of beliefs is a better asset for leadership.

Like a John Wayne, the presence of Reagan was greater than the actual Reagan. (Does anyone know whether the "Duke," away from the camera, was brave?) Reagan was greater than the sum of his parts, but Bush was less than the sum of his parts. Bush was a genuine naval hero in World War II, while Reagan was doing training films in Culver City. Bush was a warden and vestryman in his Episcopal church. Reagan talked more about God but went to church less. Bush could recite the Little League batting averages of his grandchildren, while Reagan might have to think a second to give their names. George Bush was the man you would choose to be best man at your wedding, godfather of your child, board member of your hospital, and executor of your estate.

Much has been made of George Bush's comment, "enough of that vision thing." I heard something along those lines when I drafted a speech for him in 1979. His precise words were, "Jamie, I'm a Republican—isn't that enough? Bill Buckley is a good friend of mine, and he could write *God and Man at Yale,* and I like Barry Goldwater, but stuff like his *Conscience of a Conservative* isn't my thing."

When Bush told that to me, I was in the Brook Club in New York, in a brownstone building and just as English as London's Whites or Boodles. I was drafting a speech signaling Bush's candidacy in 1980. We were talking over the tenor of his upcoming talk to the Detroit Economic Club (a command appearance for any presidential hopeful).

Bush was adamant on one point—he would reduce spending. I knew that for a politician, a promise to cut spending had all the credibility of a fat man like myself pledging to lose twenty pounds. A writer has to put teeth in such a vow. So I wrote, "On January 21, 1981, at 12:01 P.M., I will issue an executive order freezing the government payroll." (The same technique was wielded by Senator Phil Gramm in his presidential announcement speech in 1995. In an address that I worked on, Gramm promised to eliminate "set-aside" quotas in an executive order the first day.)

Of course, Bush's "Read my lips, no new taxes," was a winning ploy in his victorious election in 1988—just as his violation of that pledge would lead to his defeat in 1992. In 1988, Peggy Noonan, the writer, and Roger Ailes, the media consultant, overrode the advice of Darman, who three years later, would convince Bush to break the pledge. I'm convinced that if Lee Atwater, the campaign genius of the 1988 campaign, had lived, Bush would never have broken that vow.

In 1979, when I was going over the proposed speech with George Bush at the Brook, we decided to break at one o'clock for lunch. Bush turned down my invitation to eat at the big common table on the second floor. "Jamie, let's go to the Burger King around the corner." Bush didn't want to meet some of his old acquaintances from Greenwich, Andover, and Yale who still call him "Poppy." When the club president, "Headmaster" Frick, asked him to join the Brook, he said, "If I lose in 1980, I'll do it. (Since he went on the ticket as Reagan's vice president, he never joined, but his son Marvin did in 1995.)

In working with Bush, one noticed his eyes either flashed with intensity or glazed over with indifference. It all depended on whether you had engaged his competitive instinct or bored him with rhetorical details. (In contrast, Nixon's eyes manifested a shrewd, calculating, and cautious gaze. Reagan's, on the other hand, were always twinkling.)

If Reagan was an actor, Bush, former All-American first baseman for Yale, was an athlete. In a room, he would never sit but nervously pace with coiled-up energy. Bush, whether at tennis or horseshoes, hated to lose. That's why I discount the talk that he really wasn't trying in 1992. Bush is a compulsive competitor. (Former White House aides tell me that the medicine he was taking for his thyroid condition chemically dulled his intensive temperament.)

When Steven Provost, a fine wordsmith for Governor Tom Kean, joined the Bush campaign in September 1992, he asked me how to deal with Bush. I told him, "Steve, when you first see him, tell him you already jogged a mile that morning." Bush thinks those who are physically sharp are mentally fit. By that criteria, I flunked. That jock attitude also prevails in the corporate world, which I have learned to my detriment.

To Bush—like most CEO's—speeches were chores. He liked speaking as much as I like an exercise machine. Only on few occasions, such as an inaugural or a convention acceptance speech, did his competitive juices stir. His acceptance speech in New Orleans in 1988 and his inaugural ("a thousand points of light") would surpass those of Clinton four years later. For those addresses, he rehearsed under Roger Ailes's guidance.

One other speech I wrote for Bush in 1979 almost ended in disaster, at least for me. It was in Indianapolis in March during the time of the final four playoffs in that city for college basketball. It was unseasonably hot (87 degrees), and the Hyatt's air-conditioning was not yet turned on for the summer months. After working with Bush in his hotel room, I left for my own next door. I stripped to the buff and lay down on my bed. I was wakened by what I thought was a call for me. I got to the door, heard nothing, so I opened it a bit and stepped out to listen better. Suddenly, the door was blown shut.

There I was, locked outside my door—totally nude! I could see the newspaper headlines: "BUSH AIDE CAUGHT FLASHING." Like many Hyatts, the hotel rooms enclose a huge atrium. Protected by the chest-high rail, I signaled desperately to a waiter I saw fifteen floors below, pointing a finger (like a gun to my head) and drawing my hand across my throat. I ducked into the little alcove into which each hotel room door was set. Finally, a waiter appeared who gave me a napkin to cover myself while he went down to fetch a key.

That Sunday night, when I had dinner with Barbara in the hotel dining room, I didn't tell her of my predicament (although I expect she would have laughed), because I couldn't be sure of her husband's reaction.

While enjoying our dessert, two middle-aged women at a nearby table kept staring at Mrs. Bush. Finally, they came over and one gushingly said, "Mrs. Bush, we think your son would make a fine president." Barbara chuckled, "I know I have white hair and a matronly figure but George is my husband." They left in embarrassment. Afterwards, Barbara said to me, "Jamie, the next time someone says that, I'm going to kill her in cold blood—the hell with the campaign."

George Bush might well reply as did Churchill when he was asked at a dinner, "Who would you like to be if you couldn't be who you are?" And he answered, "Lady Churchill's second husband."

On that note, I will add that Lady Churchill, like Barbara Bush, was a handsome woman. Incidentally, in November 30, 1966, at the London Hilton honoring her recently departed husband in a birthday celebration, I asked her, "What did you see in your husband when you first met him?" "See?" she answered imperiously. "You mean, what did I hear. A man may fall in love with what he sees, but a woman falls in love with what she hears—his plans, his dreams, his hopes."

Well, when Barbara fell in love with George, it was probably with his words, not his looks and drive.

In my opinion, I think Barbara Bush is one of the most distinguished First Ladies in history—a class act. If it had been Hillary versus Barbara in 1992, Bush would have beaten Clinton in every state, *not* excepting Arkansas.

Barbara Bush took an exacting measure of her husband's speechwriters, even if her husband took little interest in his speeches. George Bush felt one was judged by what he did, not what he said.

He agreed with what an insurance company president said to me: "What counts is the bottom line—speeches are just so much BS."

Part of his disinclination for speech-making stemmed from his patrician upbringing. Dorothy Walker Bush supposedly told her second son: "Well-bred people don't brag."

George Bush may have had compunctions about pushing his beliefs, but not Margaret Thatcher. I had the occasion once to write a draft for the "Iron Lady" in 1975. She was not pleased with my effort. She was then leader of the Conservative Party. (She did not become prime minister until the Tory Party sweep in 1979, presaging Reagan's win a year later.)

In 1975, in a curious reverse of feminism, she had just visited defeated former Prime Minister Ted Heath. Many Conservative Party members secretly voted for Heath because they thought that a woman couldn't possibly win. Then there were those, angling to succeed Heath, who told their followers to vote for Thatcher because, although they didn't want Heath to lose, they wanted him to be damaged enough that he would resign and allow their names to be put forward. To their astonishment, she won.

But in 1975, as leader of the House of Commons Conservatives, she resembled Speaker Gingrich in 1995: she was less popular than her principles. As Minister of Food in Heath's government, she had been tagged "Margaret Thatcher, the Milk-Bottle Snatcher" and was portrayed by the press almost like a "Mommie Dearest" type. In contrast, Jim Callaghan, the Labourite prime minister, could have passed for a Boston bartender—not unlike a Tip O'Neill.

Bill Shelton, Thatcher's private parliamentary assistant, had met me because we both shared the experience of being English-speaking Union Scholars in the 1950s. He said, "James, write a speech showing Margaret as a housewife, shopper, and mother, with homey examples of her in the grocery store or diapering her child." Mrs. Thatcher had this comment on my draft:"Whoever tries to write for me should first read Hayek's *Road to Serfdom!*"

Margaret Thatcher has little time for fools and a long memory for foes. In 1993, at a dinner, former UN Ambassador Jean Kirkpatrick asked me if she could be introduced to Margaret Thatcher. Thatcher answered in a clipped voice, "I think not." She had remembered Kirkpatrick's opposition to the British rescue of the Falklands in 1982.

If *Road to Serfdom* was Thatcher's bible, Pat Robertson preferred the genuine article. I drafted some speeches for him when the televangelist began testing the political waters for his presidential candidacy. Robertson has about as much need for a speechwriter as he does counseling on its delivery. Yet, like those who are good at golf but buy every new book on improving their golf game, powerful speakers are always looking for ways to improve themselves.

It's a political curiosity that three senators who were congenial colleagues in the 1950s would all have sons who would run for president in 1988: Prescott Bush of Connecticut, Alvin Gore of Tennessee, and Willis Robertson of Virginia.

An additional trivia question is this: which presidential candidate in 1988 had a great-grandfather who was president of the United States? The answer, of course, is Pat Robertson. His great-grandfather was Benjamin Harrison. For one of Robertson's foreign policy speeches, I used President Harrison's statement, "The United States should not play the role of world policeman."

His antecedents include two presidents and two signers of the

Declaration of Independence. Robertson, like Churchill, who is kin to the duke of Marlborough, boasts a more patrician lineage than Bush.

But my biggest surprise in visiting him at his Virginia City headquarters was his knowledge of history and economics, his grasp of world affairs, and his proficiency in languages. He can rattle off the last year's trade figures of Brazil or the key figures in the history of Ethiopia. It helps, too, that he has been to those and many other countries.

When you meet him, he displays the same folksy affability you see on television, but the warmth cools when matters turn to the business at hand. He is driven by a mission. Though he doesn't talk Jesus to political professionals, he doesn't hide his conviction that America is "God's chosen instrument" in history, just as Israel was. For someone who is often labeled anti-Semitic, he is in fact a Zionist who counts Menachem Begin a close friend. (He even wrote a letter asking for the pardon of Jonathan Pollard, the American who was sentenced for passing secrets to Israel.)

When you talk to Pat Robertson today, it is hard to imagine that he was once a fraternity hell-raiser at Washington and Lee and a macho Marine. It is equally difficult to keep in mind that Senator Arlen Specter and Pat Robertson both learned their constitutional law and separation of church and state from the same professor in the same class. (Today, he is part politician, part evangelist, and part business titan. He has also united the passions of both his parents.) His father was a longtime chairman of the Senate Banking Committee. His mother, who hated Washington, became a religious recluse in their home in Virginia. The son melded the vocations of both.

At least by one measure, Robertson exceeded the drawing power of any other Republican. A good quarter of the audience in speeches I monitored for him in New York, Philadelphia, and Washington were black. I talked to one of them, Horace Brown, in Washington. "Mr. Humes, Dr. Robertson is the only politician speaking to the concerns of black Christian working people. The Vernon Jordans are talking to the Mercedes-Benz crowd, and Reverend Jackson is making excuses for the druggies, rappers, and muggers. We'd go for someone like a Leon Sullivan [a minister apostle of self-help in Philadelphia] but..." and he shrugged his shoulders.

The only other Republican besides Jack Kemp who saw it as his mission to reach out to blacks was Tom Kean. If there was one word that dominated the discussion in any speeches I drafted for him as governor of New Jersey, it was "inclusive." He envisioned the American dream as "Joseph's coat of many colors."

He was fascinated, in the talk I drafted for Bill Brock, the Republican National chairman, to discover that in 1978 the first act ever passed by a Republican Congress and signed by a Republican president (Lincoln) was the Homestead Act that enabled any person—white or black, man or woman—as head of a family to carve out a stake on the frontier.

Unlike the typical moderate Republican, Kean was not shy about quoting scripture to buttress that vision. ("As that shepherd, Joel in Judea said 2,500 years ago, 'The old men shall dream dreams, and the young men shall see visions.'")

Kean is a rarity in public life—one unencumbered by ego. That is also his flaw because he lacks that neurotic compulsion to make politics (and the presidency) his all-consuming ambition. George Bush—I have on good authority—would have made Tom Kean his vice-president in 1988 if political expediency had not ruled out a moderate patrician, pro-choice, WASP from the East.

Bush did choose him to be a keynoter at the 1988 convention. Kean got boos from the pro-lifers. The boos turned to cheers with one line I crafted for that address. The Democrats in their convention a month earlier had featured a red, white, and blue decor in designer colors that looked like pink, ecru, and robin's egg teal. In referring to that Kean said, "The Republican Party does not believe in pastel patriotism."

I yelled out along with the convention crowd from my hotel room in Rio de Janeiro. (A writer never knows whether his prize lines survive the final cut.) I was in Latin America on a speaking tour to groups on behalf of the State Department, the USIA Ampart program.

I had just arrived from Argentina, where I had addressed the oldest university in the Western Hemisphere, the University of Cordoba. (I received an honorary degree and learned that the last previous American honoree was Adlai Stevenson in the 1960s.) After the address, a reporter asked me if Bush would win. I said he would, but barely. At that time he was way behind Dukakis in the polls.

My belief was reinforced by something former President Nixon said to me in March 1988. "Bush will win a third term for Reagan," he said, "but he will lose in 1992—on the economy."

A day after Desert Storm ended in March 1991, I was having lunch with Ed Cox, Nixon's son-in-law, at the Brook Club. I reminded Eddie of Nixon's prediction in the light of the new polls showing Bush with an 84 percent approval rating. Ed called his father-in-law in New Jersey. I overheard on the phone, "Bush will still lose on the economy."

A sluggish economy as well as the third party candidacy of Ross Perot and his breaking his "read my lips" tax pledge are the major causes of the Bush defeat. But another was his inability to sell himself.

I often ask my clients before I propose a draft to tell me some personal anecdotes—poignant, humorous, or meaningful—about themselves.

I asked this of former All-American, Rhodes Scholar, and corporate top executive Pete Dawkins when he was a New Jersey Senate candidate in 1990. When he said he couldn't think of any, I reminded him how in the Army-Navy game I saw him drop the opening kickoff. He wouldn't use it. His failure to use it was symptomatic of his wooden campaign, and he lost.

I wanted Bush to recount his thoughts and feelings when he was downed as a naval pilot in 1944. It was a chance for him to express his dreams and aspirations for all Americans, to speak of his marriage with Barbara, of rearing his family and starting his own business. But Bush was uncomfortable with personal observations.

In the New Hampshire primary of 1980, he could have blown out Reagan if he had said in a debate: "Reagan talks about his faith. Let me tell you, only a strong faith could have sustained me when I watched my daughter, Robin, die as I held her hand while I was reading from the Psalms: 'I shall lift up my head to the hills…'"

In 1987, I was active in Bush's PAC group drafting his early presidential announcement speeches. For his campaign in 1992, my role was peripheral, working part-time with James Pinkerton on issues. (The six-foot seven-inch Pinkerton is as long in ideas as he is tall in stature. If Bush had listened to him and not Darman, he would have been reelected.)

But Bush never found his rhythm in the campaign. A strong stump speech never emerged. The problem was Bush, not his writers. Too often, the talks were tailored to the state or organization he was addressing and, as a result, they fell flat as the pudding served to Churchill, who remarked, "Pray, take away this pudding, it has no theme."

In 1993, I saw George and Barbara at his speech to the Eisenhower Exchange Fellowship Commission in Philadelphia. At a reception, Barbara said to me:

"First there was the defeat, and then days later George's mother died. Weeks later his favorite uncle, George Herbert Walker, died. The final blow was the death of Ranger. I walked in our bedroom to find him crying softly, holding our dead springer spaniel. His words were, 'Not Ranger, too.'"

But there was victory after defeat when his son, George, won the Texas governorship in 1994. Bush now admits, "If I hadn't lost in 1992, there wouldn't have been a Republican landslide in 1994."

Chapter Fifteen

SPEECH MAKER

Mend your speech a little
Lest it may mar your fortunes.
KING LEAR

mazingly, I was once asked to run for president. It all came
about because of a speech I gave in the White House in
December 1983.

Certain pro-Reagan fat cats had been invited to Washington to
hear a discussion of key political issues. During the three-day conference, one day was reserved for the White House. In the big auditorium on the third floor of the Executive Office Building (which
connects to the West Wing of the White House) President Reagan
and Vice President Bush, along with various cabinet members, strode
in to address the assembled participants.

The preoccupied secretaries of labor, commerce, transportation,
education, and energy, irritated at being ordered there by the White
House and Republican National chairman, each delivered about a
fifteen-minute laundry list of items their department was working
on, then exited to perfunctory applause. Even Reagan, in a rambling
discourse, lacked his usual flair.

The one exception in this calvacade of talks was yours truly. I had been asked to deliver my "Language of Leadership" talk at 3:20, in-between the attorney general and the secretary of agriculture.

The others may have been desultory in their speeches; I was determined that my talk would trigger a standing ovation. After all, if I was selling the power of speech, I had better be a powerful speaker.

Of course, it would have helped if I had the authority of a national name or the credentials of a cabinet position. But because I was sandwiched between such luminaries, I borrowed from their luster. After all, I had to be somebody if I was included in the format of this White House panel of dignitaries.

Unlike the other speakers, I used no notes and stood in front instead of behind the podium. I had to strip down Churchill's five principles for the language of leadership, which I had been given by his grandson, to fit twelve minutes.

These principles were (1) *Strong Beginning*—no opening amenities; (2) one tight *Theme*; (3) *Simple Language*—no passives or words like "interface" or "empowerment"; (4) *Word Pictures*—imagery such as "Iron Curtain" or "Summit"; (5) Emotional *Ending*—pride; hope; or love of God, country, or family. I illustrated each point with Churchillian anecdotes and applied them to advance various Republican programs.

I closed with this soul-shaker.

In February 1965, I saw General Eisenhower, and I asked him what were the most moving moments of the memorial services for Sir Winston Churchill the month before.

And Eisenhower replied that it was the hymn at the close of the service, Churchill's favorite anthem, the one his American mother had taught him, "The Battle Hymn of the Republic." "We all know," Eisenhower continued, "the first verse 'Mine eyes have seen the glory...' but do you know the third verse? Because

there I was seated with heads of state—Charles de
Gaulle of France, Queen Juliana of the Netherlands,
King Olav of Norway, King Baudoin of Belgium, heads
of nations whose freedom had been redeemed by the
warrior who lay in state only yards before us:

"And I could see feelings of gratitude and reverence
mist their eyes as they did my own as we all sang:

'He sounded forth the trumpet that never called
retreat.

His will goes marching on.'

And let each of us in our own communities sound
back the trumpet for the Republican and American way
of life."

The audience was silent and then stood, applauding.

A month later, I had a call from Michigan. The voice said, "May I
call you Jim? [People who don't know me always call me Jim.] I heard
you in December at the White House, and I'd like to talk to you at
your convenience."

Over dessert, he said, "Jim, do you think Reagan is going to run
again?" I said, "Yes, but I don't think it's a foregone conclusion."

"If he doesn't, who will?"

"George Bush would have the best shot for it, although I think
he'd have opposition."

He switched tack. "Jim, are you a Christian—I mean a believing
Christian?"

"Yes."

"Have you ever thought of running for president?"

"I'm a patriot," I replied stentoriously.

"Yes," was the response. "I know you are, that's why I'm here."

"Well," I wise-cracked, "I'm afraid I'm too much a patriot to
inflict myself upon the country."

That signaled the end of any presidential discussion. It turned out he represented a group of wealthy "born-agains" who were looking for someone to espouse conservative values. They had never taken an interest in politics until 1980. They were looking, in his words, for "a Christian who could talk."

A group of them, after comparing my performance with that of the cabinet members, had sent him to check me out.

If to be asked to run for president (however ridiculous the suggestion) was a high in my speech-making career, an experience a month later was a stern reminder never to believe in the hype of your own introduction.

I arrived in Corpus Christi to speak at a Texas realtors' convention. My talk was on "George Washington, First Realtor and Father of Land Development." I was met at the airport by one of those obscene long white limos and taken to a big downtown hotel.

At the hotel check-in counter, I had to give my Visa card (for incidental charges) even though the association was picking up my room bill. The bellman took me up to the Presidential Suite, a chandeliered room, wide and high enough to play basketball in. I had no sooner changed into my three-piece, pinstripe—my "speech suit"—when the phone rang.

"Dr. Humes," the voice commanded, "you are expected down immediately for the procession to the auditorium." Down in the lobby, I saw some black-garbed Texas Rangers with the mayor and the realtor association bigwigs. To the tune of Colonel Bogey's March, Bridge on the River Kwai, we began our walk through the connecting passageway from the hotel to the civic auditorium. The chamber, filled with four hundred realtors from across Texas, was dark. On a forty-yard screen behind the podium was a picture of me, as big as Mao Tse-tung.

After the invocation and the Pledge of Allegiance, I was introduced in words that would have made an egomaniac blush: "Legislator, historian, statesman, counselor of presidents, and author whose biography of Churchill was nominated for Pulitzer Prize."

About the only thing he omitted was that when I crossed the Potomac in Washington, I didn't use a bridge.

I was about ten minutes into my speech when a young hotel clerk walked in from the side of the speaker's platform and said to me:

"Mr. Humes, your Visa card is overrun—could you please come back to the desk?"

What I didn't realize until later was that hotels run your card by a computer, and if it cannot stand up to ten times the amount of your hotel room, there is an alert—another card is required.

And I was in the Presidential Suite!

I pasted a smile on my face, put an avuncular arm around the hotel clerk's shoulder, and whispered in his ear.

"Listen, if you don't want to be assigned to a Hyatt-Nome in Alaska, I suggest you return to your desk and I'll handle it later. If I walk off this platform in the middle of this talk, I guarantee you'll be lucky to be giving room service to Eskimos."

The clerk departed, and the audience waited for an explanation. "I don't care whether it's the president of the United States calling or anyone else," I said, "no one is going to make me break away from my talk to the Texas realtors." A sustained ovation was the response.

The descent from head table hero to deadbeat drone is swift. If you start believing in your own fanfare, you're a fool.

My start on the lecture circuit really began after I left the State Department in 1972. Since then, I have addressed groups in fifty states and twenty-three countries. I have talked at the White House, the Smithsonian, the steps of the Lincoln Memorial in Washington, Independence Hall in Philadelphia, the Grand Old Opry House in Nashville, Canterbury Cathedral in England, the Great Wall in China, and even the Vatican.

A friend, Joe Bongiovanni, chancellor of the Philadelphia Bar Association, wanted to return to the land of his parents with acclaim. I suggested that he purchase an option to a letter by William Paca, the only Italian signer of the Declaration of Independence.

Then with letters of invitation obtained from Mayor Frank Rizzo and President Nixon, the president of Italy was asked to come to Philadelphia for the bicentennial in 1976. We said we wanted to present him with the Paca letter.

After months with no word, we heard from the Italian ambassador in Washington that Alitalia would fly us to Rome where we would be guests of President Sergio Leone at the Palazzo Quirinale. (Incidentally, at last report, Leone was in prison for taking bribes.)

The formal invitation prompted Joe and me to engineer another invitation, one to the Vatican. We persuaded the Philadelphia cardinal to write Pope Paul and ask for a meeting. At a lunch at Castel Gondolfo, the summer Papal residence, I could only think that my Scottish Presbyterian ancestors must have been spinning in their graves.

Once my audience included two former presidents; at another, members of the British royal family; and still another, before forty Republican senators and their wives at Williamsburg.

Unless you have a household name like Colin Powell, Michael Jordan, or Diane Sawyer, lecture agencies will not be signing you up. Most lecture agencies are simply conduits to celebrities. If you lack eminence, you had better be an exciting speaker.

A Dan Rather or an Art Buchwald may deliver a boring talk, but at least the audience has the chance to see Mr. Celebrity. Who cares if they have met James Humes?

What you have to develop to be a popular speaker is what I call "the Michener method." When you finish one of his novels, you know something about Texas, Colorado, or Hawaii, and he has delivered it up with dollops of romance and adventure thrown in to make it a good read. A talk has to be both enlightening and entertaining.

The first step in giving an exciting talk is to give it an exciting title. My talk on the Gettysburg Address is "Please Don't Go to Gettysburg, Age!" Inside Story of the Gettysburg Address."

My talk on Benjamin Franklin is "What Happened at the Convention, Dr. Franklin?"

My lecture on the Royal Family is "Can God Save the Queen?"

This book is an enlargement of my talk, "Confessions of a White House Ghost."

Another trick is to write your own introduction, or you risk having the program chairman read it off your resume.

I send along an introduction with my bio. "You might find this introduction of me that was delivered recently helpful."

> As you can see, James Humes is a large man. And the scope of achievements and accomplishments is just as large. He is, or has been, a lawyer, legislator, diplomat, author, historian, actor, professor, and White House speechwriter.
>
> But whether he was arguing in court, debating in the Pennsylvania Assembly, lecturing in the University of Pennsylvania classroom, authoring twenty books, acting on stage and television, serving as a Woodrow Wilson Fellow at the Center for International Scholars at the Smithsonian, or drafting a presidential Inaugural Address, two passions dominated—a love of history and a love for the English language.
>
> That is why it comes as no surprise that his hero is Winston Churchill, whom he met, whose family he knows, whom he has portrayed on stage, and about whom he has written three books.
>
> I present to you James Humes on "The Sir Winston Method—The Language of Leadership."

But on one occasion, I was unprepared for the opening preliminaries. At Fudan University in Shanghai in 1985, I was to deliver my address: "Richard Nixon: From Chiang Kai-shek Advocate to Chou En-lai Admirer." Before I spoke, one of my hosts rose and delivered a fifteen-minute speech in Chinese. It was followed by applause which I heartily joined in until an American Embassy diplomatic aide nudged me, "I wouldn't do that, Mr. Humes. You are applauding your own introduction."

Sometimes, the less introduction the better. In April 1994, Ambassadors Walter and Lee Annenberg (she was chief of protocol under Reagan) invited me out to their Palm Springs desert estate. General Colin Powell and I were both overnight guests. Because Churchill is a great hero of General Powell, I was asked to deliver my "Never Give Up" address after a sumptuous meal. The other guests who drove over for the evening were former President Gerald Ford; former Secretary of State George Schultz; former Ambassador to the Court of St. James, Charles Price; and William Bechtel of Bechtel Industries.

As Walter Annenberg escorted me from the dining room to the living room fireplace (which was flanked by Van Goghs), he said, "James, how do you want me to introduce you?" I answered, "Walter, I want no introduction. I'm afraid my overpowering credentials might make members of this audience feel self-conscious."

"If you say so, James," replied Annenberg ponderously. The next morning the newspaper delivered to my guest room cited a poll suggesting that Powell was the most admired man in American in terms of integrity and character.

Before I sat down to join the Powells for breakfast, I made a point of studying the top of Powell's head.

"What are you looking for?" asked Powell.

"The halo."

Alma, Powell's wife, shot back, "I assure you, Jamie—it isn't there. For one thing" she said laughing, "what do you think of a husband who gives an iron to his wife for an anniversary present?"

A SPEAKER MUST ALWAYS be sensitive to local customs—particularly when speaking in foreign countries. In Papua, New Guinea, in 1983, I was asked to address a village. The invitation read that I was to be the feature offering at this ceremonial feast. (I was a little nervous. At 250 pounds, might I have been the entree?)

I pondered what I should wear at the ceremony where I was to be made honorary chieftain. I opted in this equatorial climate for my blue blazer and tan chino slacks. As it turned out, I was underdressed from the waist up and overdressed from the waist down. My chieftain host wore top hat and cutaway tails, but from the belt down he was in his altogether—totally nude!

On another occasion, I was with the prime minister of New Zealand in 1983. John Muldoon had been commanded by his doctors to lose a hundred pounds. At our lunch, I ate while he sipped a straw through his wired jaw.

At one point, he challenged me on the Balanced Budget Amendment. I told him that I reluctantly supported it.

"But why?" he asked. "It undermines parliamentary authority. The amendment is a ridiculous device—Congress only has to stop spending."

"Sir," I replied, "if I may respectfully say so, that device in your mouth is a ridiculous device. You only have to stop eating."

If that seemed intentionally rude, I was unintentionally rude on another occasion in 1982, in Madison, Wisconsin. I arrived late because of plane delays, to speak to the Rotary Club. My subject was "Churchill and the English Language." I entered as dessert was being served. I talked about Churchill, who coined such phrases as "Iron Curtain," "Summit conference," and "destroyer." Another word that Churchill added to the dictionary was : "quisling," a synonym for traitor. I quoted Churchill, saying "these vile quislings in our midst," and I added, "the way he spat out the word 'quisling,' one could almost imagine something serpentine slithering across the grass."

When I finished there was a stony silence. The chairman then announced, "We will now present the Silver Certificate of Service to the Community to Dr. Norge Quisling."

He was a second cousin of Vidkun Quisling, the Norwegian Nazi collaborator!

The only other more embarrassing situation happened in Newport, Rhode Island, a year later. I was to speak at the Naval War College in the afternoon. In the morning I came down in the Sheraton-Newporter for breakfast and heard a voice, "James Humes—will you join me?"

I immediately recognized the face of my breakfast host, but I couldn't come up with the name of the distinguished man with a Norfolk tweed jacket and paisley ascot knotted at his neck. As an old politician, I always compensated for lack of name with fulsome affection. "Well," I beamed, "you're looking more distinguished than ever."

"Remember when we first met, James, it was at the Ritz in London—you were writing a book on Churchill."

"Yes," I answered, "he Ritz—great hotel—by the way my book on Churchill is now being released in paperback."

By the time of the second cup of coffee, I had run out of chit-chat with my breakfast mate of the familiar face. So I trotted out the old gambit, "Tell me, how's the family?"

As soon as the words were out of my mouth, I simultaneously noted his stunned look and recognized him. It was Claus von Bulow, who was in Newport for the trial for allegedly trying to poison his wife—an indictment supported by the children of his wife. It was like saying, "Mrs. Lincoln, did you enjoy the play?"

Not far from the Ritz Hotel on London's Piccadilly is the English-Speaking Union (ESU), which was my club during my year in England. Ten years later, it sponsored my first speaking tour. Governor Scranton had deputized me to represent him at the renaming of Slough Grammar School to the William Penn School, since the founder of Pennsylvania had gone there in the 1630s.

Around that address the ESU had organized a series of twenty talks on "The 'State' of America" to various civic clubs. In Liverpool, I was introduced by the colorful Socialist member Bessie Braddock.

Bessie was a two-hundred-pound favorite of the union halls who would inveigh against the Tory Party in a screech worthy of a dockside fishmonger. Bessie (who liked Churchill personally) told me of her celebrated encounter with the prime minister in 1955, which I was the first to relay to American audiences. As Bessie waddled down the aisle for a division vote in 1955, she collided with a wobbly Churchill. "Winston, you are drunk," she said.

"Yes, Bessie," replied Churchill, "and you are ugly, but tomorrow I shall be sober."

A week after my speech in Liverpool, I was introduced in Stratford-upon-Avon by another member of Parliament, as different from Bessie as a Rolls Royce from a fiver tugboat—John Profumo. The Conservative member from Warwickshire, Profumo was a taller and more handsome version of Sir Laurence Olivier. Profumo said, "As the member from Stratford-upon-Avon, it might be appropriate to conclude my introduction of the Honorable James Humes with the words of the Bard about Sir John Falstaff: 'You are a gentleman of excellent breeding and admirable discourse.'" (Profumo, a defense minister, would resign his seat a week later because he lied about his affair with Mandy Davies. Davies was also sleeping with a Russian agent.) The controversy swirling about him at the time in no way diminished the effect on his Shakespeare-laden introduction.

The most ringing introduction I ever had came in that same tour at the Carmen dinner in London's Guild Hall. Carmen referred not to the opera but to the carriage drivers in the fourteenth century when the guild began. The guild is almost Masonic in its rites and ceremonies. In the twentieth century, it has become (by invitation only) the trade association of Britain's motor industry. Still others are inherited legacies.[5]

---

[5] As an honorary member, I have prized and exercised one privilege: A Carmen is the only Englishman who can with impunity urinate beside his car. It dates from the days when a carriage driver could not leave his horses unattended. My wife, however, does not think the right extends to this country.

On the morning of the noontime feast, it was pointed out to me that my name was in the Court Circular corner of the *London Times* along with the historian, Sir Arthur Bryant, and the Earl of Tunis, Field Marshal Alexander. I repaired to my room at the ESU on Charles Street to polish my sententious remarks on Anglo-American relations.

Just after our preprandial sherry, the lord mayor and other head table guests were ushered into an antechamber. At 1:30 the toastmaster, not in the American meaning, looking like a model for Beefeater Gin, stentoriously blared:

"THE HONOURABLE REPRESENTATIVE JAMES CALHOUN HUMES."

After the other two chief honorees delivered their after-dinner remarks, I realized that an after-dinner speech is not a talk after dinner, but a form as stylized as a sonnet. It calls for humor followed by a short sentimental or serious commentary.

So, I scrapped my original remarks and told of my visit to Runnymede four years before.

> While my wife and I readied ourselves to hear the guide lecture to visiting tourists on that epic confrontation of King John with the Barons, a tour bus arrived. An American garbed in a Hawaiian sport shirt and blue trousers and carrying a camera helped his wife, whose beam filled ample aquamarine slacks, down the bus steps.
>
> Just at that point the Runnymede tour guide intoned, "In 1215 King John signed the Magna Carta…"
>
> Upon hearing that the American wife exclaimed "Elmer, we missed it by twenty minutes."

Then, starting with the Magna Carta, I paid tribute to the habeas corpus, petition of right, and other title deeds of common heritage. The high point of my ESU speaking tour was attending the

Conservative Party Conference in Blackpool. I didn't orate there, I observed. That conference in October 1963 was the only British party conference in recent history that looked like an American political convention.

On the eve of the conference, the ailing Harold Macmillan announced his retirement as prime minister and as leader of the Conservative Party. Close to a majority of the members wanted "R.A.B." Butler, who had been passed over in 1957 in favor of Macmillan through the maneuverings of retired Prime Minister Churchill. But the local chairmen party agents in the constituency preferred the robust Tory Blue conservatism of Lord Hailsham to Butler's "pinkish" variety.

I was to join Randolph Churchill for dinner to hear Party Chairman Ian McLeod. Afterward, I wandered down to the docks. There, I found Randolph Churchill with socks and shoes off, sobering himself up in the tides of the North Sea. He wore on his jacket a huge pin in the shape of the letter Q.

"James," he said, "last time I told them it wouldn't be Butler but Mac [Macmillan], and this time it will be Quentin."

He then proceeded to excoriate Butler as a former Chamberlain-type appeaser. "He's such a trimmer—he'd trim off edges of the Union Jack."

By the way, earlier that year Randolph had gone to the hospital to have a lump removed. When it was found to be benign, MacLeod commented, "Amazing, they found the only thing in Randolph's body that was not malign."

Incidentally, Randolph's son, Winston, once told me, "Actually, James, father was a better extemporaneous speaker than grandfather."

The answer of course is that Randolph had inherited more of his father's brilliance than of his character.

Years later, his son Winston told me about the last time he saw his father. At East Bergholt in Sussex, Winston said to his bedridden parent, "Father, they just got the man who got Robert Kennedy."

The dying Randolph whispered, "Why haven't they found the man who got me?" The answer was himself.

In 1963, Randolph Churchill's candidate, Quentin Hogg, did not succeed Macmillan. Neither was it "Rab" Butler. Instead, it was my distant kin and head of the Hume, Home, and Humes clan, the Earl of Home (pronounced Hume), who had been serving as Macmillan's foreign secretary. My last contact with Home and his family was just after my wedding (complete with kilt and bagpipes) in Duddingston.

Three years later, I was a guest at the Beefsteak Club in London. The club, among other things, is noted for the invention of the sandwich. A member, Lord Sandwich, devised the combination of meat between bread so he could eat and play cards at the same time.

As I later learned, no one enters the dining room until three members have arrived. The third to arrive presides. This is because in the eighteenth century, a particularly garrulous member used to arrive the earliest in order to seize the presiding chair at a table set for twelve.

On that October day in 1966, I had a luncheon address at the British-American Chamber of Commerce. I had been introduced at the affair by my friend, Sir John Wedgwood, of the noted pottery family, whom I had met and stayed with on my trip three years before.

Sir John, who knew I relished the intricate traditions of London Club life, had taken me as a guest to this historic club.

Leading me, the sixty-year-old Wedgwood bounded up the stairs. But upon entering, his energy as well as his customary enthusiasm vanished. I was seated at the second chair to the left of the "presider," and after Wedgwood mumbled my name to the man on my immediate left, he turned for the rest of the dinner and engaged raptly the member at his right.

My companion on my left and I were trapped into hearing a diatribe against General Alexander's campaign in Europe by the presider, Sir James Marshall-Cornwall, a retired British general.

We left about eleven. When we returned to his flat, John explained his rudeness: "James, dreadfully sorry, but it was a very sticky wicket. I didn't want to make introductions because I was terribly afraid that Lord Cornwall would remember me.

"I've come to the club for years, James," Wedgwood continued, "but this was the first time since 1938 that I'd seen him. I had come down [graduated] from Cambridge and was working for British intelligence.

"It was arranged that I would meet his daughter and after a few—what do you Americans call it—"dates," I was invited down to his country home for a weekend. There, after everyone was asleep, I searched and photographed the papers in his desk.

"You see, James, letters from German Foreign Secretary Von Ribbentrop had been intercepted which revealed that Cornwall, a pro-Munich appeaser, was recommended as a possible front man in case of German occupation. Except for some diatribes found in the correspondence hoping that 'Hitler would take care of the Bolsheviks', there was nothing that really indicated that he was anything less than a patriot.

"Yet, his career was ruined. He would have headed the African campaign against Rommel. Instead, he was assigned some governorship of an obscure British island for the war's duration."

Having attended the British Conservative Party Conference in October 1963, the National Republican Convention in August 1964, and then the Canadian Conservative Conference in Ottawa in December 1964, I had the unique experience of seeing the three parties of the right in the English-speaking world pass through times of self-examination as they pondered their future course.

My experience in Ottawa was the only time I played a role in the politics of another nation. I had been invited to address the Young Conservative at the Chateau Laurier Hotel in Ottawa. My topic was "Today or Tomorrow: Survival or Revival."

Having just been defeated for reelection, I said that hundreds of

Republican legislators like myself would not have been defeated had the Republican presidential candidate been a moderate of the Eisenhower-Nixon stripe, but that Goldwater's principled conservatism would make Republicans the party of the future.

To my surprise, I was invited after my talk by Dalton Camp, the party chairman, to sit in on the Executive Conference, open only to Conservative members of Parliament or provincial party officers. Most of the speeches involved the usual reports until Leon Balcer, a member of Parliament from one of the maritime provinces, rose and attacked John Diefenbaker, former prime minister and then leader of the opposition. Diefenbaker, he charged, was the cause of the defeats in recent by-elections. He then made the almost unprecedented motion that Diefenbaker should resign as leader. A hush fell over the audience as other members rose to support Balcer's motion.

Diefenbaker was a prairie lawyer, whose path to party leadership had been blazed by his populist oratory. In 1958, he led the Progressive Conservative to their first national victory in thirty years. But by 1964, the party had lost its majority in the House of Commons. He was a Dirksen when the style of Kennedy was in fashion.

Diefenbaker was not at the conference ballroom, but his handpicked chairman of the party, Dalton Camp, was, and he had the task of quelling the insurrection.

Suddenly, Camp announced, "Ladies and Gentlemen, I must interrupt to say that I invited a speaker from the United States to address us, and I apologize for detaining him so long. The Honorable James Humes from Pennsylvania."

I was stunned. But I was ushered to the podium. After ten minutes I was handed a note from Camp to the lectern: "Finish your talk and sit down!"

When I sat down, Camp announced, "Ladies and Gentlemen, I am overdue five minutes for a press conference. So, I call this meeting adjourned."

As I began to leave the room, I was restrained by a Canadian mountie.

"Mr. Humes, you have been invited to Mr. Diefenbaker's house to spend the night."

"But, you see, I have this radio interview in ten minutes…"

"It has been canceled. The station was told. Come with me."

So, I spent the night at the Mansion, the house recently set aside for the leader of the opposition, and the next morning I was driven to the airport. Dalton Camp had not wanted to let me loose with any reporters who might find out about the move to oust Diefenbaker.

On that frigid December night, Mrs. Diefenbaker topped off her dinner with a chocolate cake she had baked.

When she offered me seconds, I said, "Mrs. Diefenbaker, I can't say no, it's a character fault."

"You know, James," John Diefenbaker, "that was the problem with John Kennedy. He had every criterion of leadership but one: character. He was like the icing on that cake—except there was nothing inside."

When I came home, I jotted down the chocolate cake anecdote for my files.

Sorting through anecdotes had become a formula for fashioning talks. In my recent ESU speaking tour, I hit upon this method to make my speeches entertaining as well as enlightening.

In Britain I would seize upon anecdotes about Benjamin Franklin, George Washington, or the Constitutional Convention, and to that pile I would add some of my own experiences as congressional staff member or state legislator that explained points about our separation of powers or federal government.

In other words, instead of writing out my remarks and finding anecdotes to fit, I did it backwards: gather the anecdotes first and then fit the speech around them. (I learned later that sometimes Reagan used that technique for his speech circuit.)

In 1964, I organized another speaking tour across Pennsylvania.

The American Bar Association was supporting a twenty-fourth amendment to the Constitution—the Presidential Disability Amendment. The assassination of Kennedy had reminded that James Garfield, when shot, lay thirty-one days in a coma. In this nuclear age such a scenario was impossible.

In the fifty-odd speeches I gave then, I learned another speaking trick: skip the opening amenities (e.g., It is an honor to be…).

In these talks I would open:

> Imagine for a moment the second floor of the White House where a stricken president lies, cast down by an assassin. He is in a coma. The secretary of state delays taking appropriate action in Europe…

Amenities are often banalities. The prime time for listening is just after you are introduced. That's when your audience is waiting to see what you look like and what you sound like. So, I wouldn't dissipate that psychological edge with trite inanities, not even a joke.

Instead, I devised something I called "Parenthetical Praise"—that is, in the middle of the talk I would single out certain members of the audience. In this particular talk, I might mention the names of attending lawyers, physicians, and even undertakers.

> Dr. Smith can tell you better than I that it is almost impossible to predict the length of a coma.

Invariably, those singled out were the first to congratulate me on my talk.

In the same way any extolling of the club's charitable work or town's virtues would in the middle of the talk. Praise in the beginning of the talk comes off as flattery, but in the middle as sincerity.

I would also make it a point to arrive early at the hotel where I was to make my luncheon address. The more people I could converse with beyond pleasantries the better. As I ate lunch, I would spot where those few were seated. Then in the talk I would lock them in a gaze at least once. It had the effect of making them believe I had been speaking directly to them the whole time. Again, they would be the first to applaud, and to keep applauding.

Twenty years later in Omaha, Nebraska, before a speech, I talked to one elderly lady and found out that her mother had been born in Williamsport.

I was delivering my "Never Give Up" talk on Churchill. And I engaged my new, aged acquaintance in a look from the very beginning. At the end of the talk I received a standing ovation from everyone but the lady who remained sitting in the front row. When everyone started to leave, she didn't stir. We went up to her. She had died. Talk about slaying them in the aisles.

During these ESU tours, I also learned and polished the two key techniques of persuasive platform speaking: the pause, and change of modulation. By giving the same talk over and over, the content becomes second nature and you instinctively learn when to lower your voice and pause for effect.

Still, it was not until I served my White House stints as a speechwriter that I became a polished platform performer. Until then, I spoke from notes. Afterward, I wrote out my speeches. Memorable phrases or catchy lines do not emerge from a rambling presentation.

Lincoln made notes on the back of an envelope on the train ride to Gettysburg, but the notes were serial key words and phrases to help commit to memory a speech he had been seven drafts in preparing. In the same way I drafted, revised, and polished my talk and then would memorize it by reducing it to a series of brief and briefer notes. When I came to deliver it, I spoke without a text or even notes.

As Nixon told me, "Jamie, you may forget things you wanted to say, but you more than make up for it with your direct eye contact with the audience when you're not constantly looking down at notes or text."

One final tip came from a screen star. "James," she said, "don't start speaking right after the introduction. Stop, make sure the audience is absolutely still. Count to ten, no twenty. You're big and have good stage presence—dramatize it."

The advice came from Olivia de Havilland in Newport, Rhode Island, in 1980. She and I were putting on back-to-back talks.

In my "Never Give Up" talk, I tell this story to dramatize a critical moment in Churchill's career:

> In 1931, Churchill went to America for a speaking tour that took him across the country. Afterward, he went to Calgary, Canada. Before the luncheon, a pert and pretty waitress brought him a glass of sherry. And then she proffered a glass to the Methodist bishop of Calgary, and he replied:
>
> "Young lady, I would rather commit adultery than take a glass of intoxicating spirits."
>
> Whereupon Churchill motioned to the waitress, "Lassie, lassie, come back, come back. I didn't know we had been given a choice."

In 1990, Senator Jesse Helms asked me to deliver my Churchill "Never Give Up" talk to a small group of big contributors.

I owed something to Helms because he had supported my quest for an ambassadorial appointment by President Bush in 1989. The appointment didn't work out. (One was promised if Bush was reelected in 1992.) Still, I owed Jesse and agreed to come when he asked me to talk to a certain group. Ten minutes into my Churchill spiel came the yell, "Will that goddamn Englishman sit down—we want to hear Jesse!"

So did I. Of a sudden, all eyes turned to the rear of the auditorium where a phalanx of feminists, looking like the East German Olympic field hockey team, rammed its way in. For minutes, it looked as if the good ole' boys that were mounting a defense were overmatched.

Then a local Methodist church choir tried its best but failed to drown out the shouts of the protestors and their blaring rendition of "The Battle Hymn."

Fortunately, just at that time, the U.S. cavalry arrived in the form of the senator and his entourage.

Helms began with:

> My friends, I'm delighted to see here that renowned author and scholar James Humes, the kind of statesman who should be representing our nation abroad.
>
> You know, the first thing I'm going to do in President Bush's next term is to make him our man in Malta.

Resounding cheers followed for me and the senator.

Still, it is far better to have an audience waiting to hear you and not someone else. In Brisbane, Australia, I had a standing ovation from five hundred convention delegates before I even opened my mouth. The *Brisbane Herald* said the next day, "Not since General MacArthur has a speaker so mesmerized a Brisbane audience."

As I said before, five elements comprise great eloquence: great message, great phrasing, great delivery, great occasion, and great man (or woman).

In Brisbane, I was not a great personage but I was a surrogate of one—President Reagan, via substitute Jack Kemp who had been sidetracked to deliver the keynote address to the National Party Convention.

Peter Temple-Morris, a British Conservative Party member of Parliament, was the other keynoter, deputized by Prime Minister Margaret Thatcher.

Though I stayed up most of the night to write my once-in-a-lifetime speech, I had to rush back to the hotel and revise my beginning after I heard my British counterpart in his address try to sell the new Soviet Chairman Mikail Gorbachev, in his address, as one "the West could do business with." It was the wrong speech to the wrong audience. The National Party is the more conservative of the two right-of-center parties in Australia. Peter Temple-Morris described the new kind of urbane Soviet leader. "Why, he wore Gucci shoes and used an American Express Card for his purchases when I went with him to Harrods." I alluded to the Britisher's words.

> In Russia the people have a name for the Communist Party elite, who drive in their chauffeured limousines in street lanes reserved for them only, to stores reserved for them only, and buy with credit cards reserved for them only, the Gucci shoes, Pucci ties, Dior shirts—they call them Commi-*czars* spelled C-Z-A-R-S—czars who would make the Romanovs green with envy.
>
> And if Gorbachev and his ilk want to deal, it is not because they are peaceful, but because they are panicked. They see not only the writing on the wall, but the crumbling of the wall—the Berlin Wall and the other walls of the Iron Curtain that have kept their people from freedom.

After Temple-Morris's nouvelle-cuisine speech, mine was red meat for the ravenous. The "public-school" plummy-toned English Parliamentarian with his Oxford accent was the personification of the "Pommie" that the Aussies dislike. They feel those Brits are looking down on their outcast lineage. Unlike their New Zealand neighbors, they prefer the Yanks to the Brits.

In Australian lore, the greatest idol comes not out of politics but of sports—and he is not a human but a horse. I set up this allusion to the Phar Lap, their legendary race horse.

I closed with this "soul shaker" story of the last time General Eisenhower saw Winston Churchill:

> In the summer of 1964, General Eisenhower came to Europe for ceremonies commemorating D-Day. Afterward he called on the dying Winston Churchill in King George V Hospital in London.
>
> Churchill, his body enfeebled by the infirmities of nine decades, lay propped up on the bed. Suddenly, his face illuminated with the recognition of Eisenhower at the door, and he extended his pink cherubic hand to enclasp Eisenhower's seated at the bedside.
>
> Four minutes passed—no words spoken, just two old men holding hands sharing silently the memories of battles they together fought for ideals they mutually cherished.
>
> Eight minutes passed—no words, except perhaps by Churchill himself, could surpass the poignancy and eloquence of the mute handclasp between two nations, two leaders… two friends.
>
> Fourteen minutes passed—no words spoken, and then Churchill unclasped the hand and gently waved with his in a V sign.
>
> Eisenhower withdrew. Outside, he saw his son and said, "Johnny, I just said goodbye to Winston, but you know you never say farewell to courage."
>
> And in a Queenslander, there are no constraints on courage.

It was a tear-jerker, and it jerked the Brisbane audience to its feet. When the ovation subsided, a delegate offered the resolution that "James Humes be elected Honorary Chairman of the National Party for life." It passed by acclamation.

As a boy, I fantasized delivering the keynote address to resounding cheers at a national convention. In a sense I fulfilled the dream—except it was not in America but in Australia!

INDEX

211

8/30